A Global Ethic

The Leadership Challenge

WILLIAM D. HITT

✳ BATTELLE PRESS

Columbus • Richland

Library of Congress Cataloging-in-Publication Data

Hitt, William D.
   A global ethic : the leadership challenge / by William D. Hitt
      p.   cm.
   Includes bibliographical references and indexes
   ISBN 1–57477–016–0 (alk. paper)
      1. Ethics. 2. Values—Psychological aspects. 3. Social values—
   Psychological aspects. 4. Leadership—Moral and ethical aspects.
   5. Life. I. Title.
   BJ1012.H58 1996
   170'.44—dc20   96-7023
                                                      CIP

Printed in the United States of America

Copyright © 1996 Battelle Memorial Institute

Battelle Press
505 King Avenue
Columbus, OH 43201-2693
614–424–6393
1–800–451–3543
Fax: 614–424–3819

In memory of

KARL JASPERS

who provided the foundation.

The compass that we have used as a logo on the front of the book is the classic symbol of the ethicists' search for moral direction. Thanks to Fred W. Friendly, Columbia University Seminars on Media and Society.

CONTENTS

Synopsis   xi

I.   WHY A GLOBAL ETHIC?   1

II.   THE FRAMEWORK   11

III. THE FULLY FUNCTIONING PERSON   35

IV.   WAY TO WISDOM   81

V.   THE GOOD LIFE   103

VI.   A GLOBAL COMMUNITY   129

      Exercises   157

      Suggested Readings   165

      Bibliography   167

      Name Index   177

      Subject Index   181

Your life is your message. Leadership by example is not only the most pervasive but also the most enduring form of leadership. And because the world is becoming more interconnected, standards of leadership have an impact that extends around the globe. Now, as never before, a higher standard of leadership will serve us all.

KESHAVAN NAIR
A Higher Standard of Leadership:
Lessons from the Life of Gandhi

ACKNOWLEDGMENTS

I am indebted to a number of people for helping me bring this book into being. It would be impossible to name them all, but I want to acknowledge a select few.

I owe more than I can possibly say to Karl Jaspers, the philosopher who has had a deep and lasting impact on my life and thought. As my mentor, Karl Jaspers taught me how to center my life in the atrium of the temple. Much of what is contained in *A Global Ethic* can be traced either directly or indirectly to the writings of this renowned philosopher.

For reviewing and critiquing the manuscript, I am indebted to my colleagues Cameron Fincher, Irene Hays, Jon Olson, and Gerry Robinson. They were able to look from the outside in and identify my blind spots as well as enhance my seeing spots. Their insight and acumen contributed substantially to improving the manuscript.

Yvonne Burry is the editor *par excellence*. Her sharp eye and astuteness enhanced the readability of the manuscript immeasurably.

My secretary, Jean Hayward, was able to convert handwritten material into a beautifully typed manuscript. As we endeavored to continually improve the manuscript, she made numerous revisions—with great patience and understanding.

For final editing, I would like to thank Beatrice Weaver. Her sharp eye enhanced the quality of the manuscript.

I also am greatly indebted to Joe Sheldrick, the editor of Battelle Press. Getting a typed manuscript into book form and out to the marketplace requires considerable management and organization know-how. The editor of Battelle Press has this know-how in great measure.

To each and every one of these persons, I want to express my sincere thanks.

SYNOPSIS

Kurt Lewin, the social psychologist, never tired of saying, "There is nothing so practical as a good theory." In like manner, we can say, "For anyone working in the international community, there is nothing so practical as a global ethic."

PRESENT SITUATION

An increasing number of leaders in the world community have begun to recognize the need for a global ethic. They understand the need for a set of moral principles that would be generally accepted by the peoples of the world. They pose this question: What are the universal values that will provide a moral compass?

We can liken the present world situation to an archway that leads into the temple. The well-hewn stones of the archway represent the global issues that are now linking the peoples of the world: the global economy, the global environment, global security, global law, and global communication. A global ethic is not another stone alongside these five, but, to borrow a phrase from Rousseau, it is "the keystone to the archway." This keystone supports all the other stones. Without the keystone, the archway will collapse.

In our efforts to illuminate the nature of the keystone, we must find commonality within diversity. With so many nations, so many cultures, so many religions, so many philosophies, so many business practices, where do we find the common ground? Where do we find the core universal values that will provide the moral compass?

PROPOSITION

Richard Tarnas, in *The Passion of the Western Mind*, states it well when he says:

> Since evidence can be adduced and interpreted to corroborate a virtually limitless array of world views, the human challenge is to engage that world view or set of perspectives which brings forth the most valuable, life-enhancing consequences.

In support of this idea of "life-enhancing consequences," our basic proposition is that we should select the world view that focuses primarily on promoting human flourishing. The Latin for flourish is *florere*, formed on the root *flor* for flower. Thus, the meaning of flourish is to bloom, to thrive, to prosper, to be fully developed—i.e., to become fully human.

This basic proposition then leads to a terse definition of good and evil. *Good* is that which enhances human flourishing; *evil* is that which thwarts human flourishing. This definition applies to people in all cultures in all times. It is truly universal.

PRINCIPLES

The one world view that has human flourishing as its principal aim is Humanitas. The Latin meaning of *humanitas* is "human nature or character." The roots of the word denote (1) the quality distinguishing civilized people from savages and beasts and (2) humane character, kindness, human feeling. It seems reasonable to suggest that the word "humanity" focuses on what humankind *is* and the word "humanitas" focuses on what humankind *can become*—in a very positive sense. In other words, *humanity* concentrates on human actuality and *humanitas* concentrates on human potentiality.

The realization of human potentiality through human flourishing can be achieved—on a global scale—only if the peoples of the world view themselves as members of a global community, as a multitude of diverse cultures with a common center. And a *sine qua non* of a global community is a global ethic—the keystone that reflects universal moral values.

Thus, in a nutshell, this is the Humanitas philosophy:

1. The *meaning* of Humanitas: the quality that separates civilized people from savages and beasts.

2. The *aim* of Humanitas: promoting human flourishing for the people of the world, including both present and future generations.

3. The *way* of Humanitas: building a global community grounded in a global ethic.

PROPOSAL

We know that building a global community will depend on the members of that community agreeing on a common ethic. And we also know that furthering a common ethic will depend on the leaders in the world community being infused with that ethic. By "leaders," we mean individuals who are able to influence the thoughts, feelings, and/or behavior of others. They can be at any level in the organization and in any type of organization—governmental, non-governmental, or transnational corporations.

The Humanitas global ethic holds out to leaders in these organizations five leadership challenges:

1. *Find the common ground by being a citizen of the world.*
   The essence of being a citizen of the world is a sense of oneness with the human family. And there is no inherent conflict in dual citizenship: Every leader can be a proud citizen of both his/her nation of origin and the world community.

2. *Strive to become a fully functioning person and to help others become fully functioning persons.*
   These two aims are synergistic. By becoming a fully functioning human being, the leader is likely to enhance the personal development of others. And by enhancing the personal development of others, the leader is very likely to elevate his or her own personal development.

3. *Live a life of total dedication to the truth, to the* whole *of truth.*
   What can we know? We can know truth. And what is truth? Truth is conformity to what is real or actual. Even though reality is ever-changing and we can never grasp it completely, we nevertheless can have an unconditional commitment to the quest for truth.

4. *Be truly committed to the good life.*
   This means, in essence, to do good and avoid evil. Do what you can to enhance human flourishing and avoid thwarting human flourishing—both your own and that of others.

5. *Enlist others to be citizens of the world.*
   Just suppose that each leader in the world community would become a citizen of the world and then enlist ten

other persons to become citizens of the world. Each of these ten others would then enlist ten others, and on and on. . . . What a transformation we would witness in the world community!

PROSPECTS

These five guiding principles capture the gist of the Humanitas global ethic. But note that these principles are not all-inclusive, nor do they account for the multitude of culture-specific moral values found around the world. Nevertheless, they should serve as a bare-minimum set of universal standards: a set of core values that would be agreed upon by leaders of good will, regardless of nationality, ethnicity, or religion.

Kant expressed it well: "If each person would clean up his own yard, the whole world would be clean." And so it is with these five guiding principles. If each leader in the world community would abide by these principles, we would have an ethical world. A Utopian notion, of course. But each step in that direction would be a small victory. As Seneca, the Roman philosopher, so aptly stated, "We cannot eliminate evil from the world, but we can prevent its victory."

It all boils down to the following logic: Human flourishing on a global scale will depend heavily on building a global community . . . and building a global community will depend heavily on framing a generally acceptable global ethic. Going in reverse order: Framing a global ethic will contribute substantially to building a global community . . . and building a global community will contribute substantially to human flourishing. Given this logic, one can readily understand why a global ethic is the keystone to the archway.

In sum, this is the Humanitas story. And the story can become a reality in locales around the world, from Scotland to South Africa to Bangladesh. And not only *in* locales but *between* locales. It all depends on the will of leaders in the world community to translate concept into practice.

For the reader of *A Global Ethic*, these are the desired outcomes:

1. Why a Global Ethic?: an understanding of the need for a global ethic

2. The Framework: an understanding of how the primary world views can be integrated into a framework for a global ethic

3. The Fully Functioning Person: an understanding of what it means to be a fully functioning human being

4. Way to Wisdom: an understanding of different paths to truth and how all paths are anchored in mental models

5. The Good Life: an understanding of the universal attributes of the good life

6. A Global Community: an understanding of what will be required to build a global community and the key leadership role.

Exercises: a demonstration of the above understanding by responding to focused questions.

If, as a result of reading and reflecting on this book, you begin to see yourself as a citizen of the world—as one who can have a significant impact on the world beyond the confines of the organizational job description—then the book will have achieved its aim.

I

WHY A GLOBAL ETHIC?

We cannot define the ultimate aim of history but we can posit an aim which is itself a premise for the realization of the highest potentialities. And that is *the unity of mankind*.

KARL JASPERS
Way to Wisdom

A global ethic? A set of moral principles that would provide a common center for the peoples of the world? Is it possible that we might frame an ethic for the peoples of the world—including people of all nations, of all cultures, of all religions? This is the central question addressed in *A Global Ethic*. If we look closely, we will see hints of a slowly emerging global ethic.

But, as might be expected, the skeptics will respond that all notions of a global ethic are wishful thinking, Utopian, and ignorant of the harsh realities of the everyday world. They will quickly marshal evidence to support a completely contrary point of view.

"Let's be real!" these critics will respond. Consider the numerous present-day tensions between nations: we find opposing beliefs, conflict, and the refusal to negotiate. Consider the different ethnic groups within a given nation: we find opposing beliefs, conflict, and the refusal to negotiate. Consider the citizens of any local community who represent different interests: we find opposing beliefs, conflict, and the refusal to negotiate. And even consider the heterogeneity among the members of a single family: even here we find opposing beliefs, conflict, and the refusal to negotiate. If this is the real world, how can we even consider the possibility of a global ethic?

Framing a global ethic means that we have found at least a foundation for common ground—an area of agreement. A global ethic would bring the peoples of the world together—at least to begin a dialogue.

Once again, the skeptics will be skeptical. "Common ground? Where? Show us." They would quickly point out events and forces around the world that highlight *uncommon ground*. And, frankly, present day facts as well as history lend credence to their charge.

The skeptics would have us take a serious look at each of the principal world views tied to religion, science, and philosophy. They are at least partially in conflict with each other— always. And the advocates of each world view will insist that theirs is the best route to truth, wisdom, and the good life. Fervent advocates probably will be unreceptive to the other world views.

A fourth world view—focusing on daily life—is perhaps closest to reality. These advocates go on their way each day coping, coping, and coping, oblivious to the theoretical arguments engaged in by the proponents of the other world views. And these people appear to be on ground different from the others.

Thus, we have four primary world views: religion, science, philosophy, and daily life—all radically different in basic assumptions and guiding principles. All with proponents who will make special note of the salient differences between and among these world views. Again, the skeptic can ask: "Where is the common ground?"

Even within each of the four world views, we find opposing points of view and frequent conflict. In religion, for example, we find Hindus opposed to Muslims, Protestants opposed to Catholics, and on and on. In philosophy, we find materialists opposed to idealists and both opposed to existentialists. In science, we find physicists at odds on how best to describe and explain the smallest of the smallest phenomena—wave theory versus particle theory. And finally, in daily life, we simply have to open our eyes and look around us to note the considerable diversity of viewpoints—from politics to education to good health. Where is the common ground?

To find the common ground, Meister Eckhart, the celebrated 14th century scholastic, persuades us that "the shell must be cracked apart if what is in it is to come out; *for if you want the kernel, you must break the shell.*" The shell symbolizes the uncommon ground, that is, diversity that is in conflict. The kernel is the common ground—which is much smaller in size. But the kernel is indeed a reality, and we must not allow the magnitude of the shell to overshadow the beauty and potential of the kernel.

The kernel represents the common ground that is of immediate and continuing concern to all the peoples of the world . . . the kernel is *the future of humanity*.

What will become of the kernel is not self-evident and it is not preordained. It can either die or flourish. Its outcome depends on what we humans decide or do not decide. The future of humanity offers humankind both threats and opportunities.

In our present era, three life-threatening forces greatly concern the world at large and will impact the future of humanity. These are environmental degradation, the threat of wars of mass destruction, and the population explosion.

With respect to environmental degradation, we are gradually becoming aware of such potential hazards as the diminishing ozone layer, rampant deforestation, acid rain, radioactive waste, and on and on. Experts may disagree on the magnitude of each particular threat, but most will agree that these critical issues deserve the attention of humanity at large.

With respect to the threat of wars of mass destruction (nuclear, chemical, biological), who can say what might happen? Even without two superpowers engaged in a Cold War and nuclear standoff, an increasing number of other nations now possess the capability for building weapons of mass destruction. Any one of these nations could trigger a regional, if not global, disaster. Other nations cannot simply stand by and wait to see what might happen.

The third life-threatening force, the population explosion, is equal in importance to the other two. Historically, the predictions of population growth are fairly accurate. At the turn of the century, the world population will be at about six billion. Then extrapolate out another 50 or 60 years forward and the estimate is 12 billion. Imagine: in one lifetime, the world population may grow from six billion people to 12 billion people. How will humanity respond to this critical issue?

Reflecting on the interconnections of these three life-threatening forces is extremely sobering. What if the world population does grow to 12 billion by 2050? What will happen to the environment, which is already being fully tested and depleted by a population of some six billion? And with an ever-increasing population clamoring for shrinking environmental resources and with the poorer nations having the capability for building weapons of mass destruction, what is the increased probability of an all-out war? Indeed, these three forces are intertwined. They are the "troubling troika" that brings the question of survival to our consciousness—especially for the survival of humanity. Further, no one of these life-threatening forces can be subdued by a single nation or even a bloc of nations. Successfully dealing with these intertwined forces demands that the peoples of the world work collaboratively. This is our common ground.

So much for the threat. What about the realm of opportunity? Here our challenge calls for the very best of humanity—both mind and spirit. Here our challenge is to unite the peoples of the world—of every nation, of every culture, of every religion—with a directive that should appeal to everyone, even the skeptics. The challenge is to focus on *the future*

5

of humanity. This is our common ground. This is how humanity can break the shell.

The discerning student of world affairs can see that the shell is susceptible to breakage. In the midst of skepticism there are forces and trends that support the possibility of a global ethic. In the political arena, for example, the United Nations has demonstrated that the member nations can convene, debate, and agree on an approach to resolving an urgent international crisis, such as the Gulf War. In religion, the Council for a Parliament of the World's Religions has shown that people of many different faiths can meet together in dialogue and agree on "An Initial Declaration of a Global Ethic." In science, we find researchers from different countries convening at international congresses to share their research findings and to launch collaborative projects. In education, innovative programs cut across national borders just as thousands of exchange students also cross national borders. In international trade, transnational corporations and nations and blocs of nations reach accord on tariffs and trade. Undergirding all of these activities is a common international access to the media—television, radio, and newspapers. Marshall McLuhan was correct when he predicted that television would transform the world of nation-states into a global village. Now with the Internet and e-mail, we have effective and instantaneous means of communication for people around the world. Enhancing the communication is the fact that English is becoming the universal language for the peoples of the world.

Given these favorable signs, the question then becomes: Why do we need a common ethic for the people of the world? The Council for a Parliament of the World's Religions provides a clear answer:

> There will be no global order without a new global ethic. . . . By a global ethic we mean a fundamental consensus on binding values, irrevocable standards, and personal attitudes.

Without such a fundamental consensus on an ethic, sooner or later every community will be threatened by chaos or dictatorship, and individuals will despair.

Few would doubt the need for building a world community—for survival, for security, and for human flourishing. And if this world community truly comes into being, it must have the underpinnings of a global ethic—core values embedded within a meaningful framework.

We can cite several examples of misguided frameworks. Religion, for example, is a framework that many people feel could provide global unity. But the history of two millennia demonstrates clearly that one particular religion cannot unite the people of the world. Then there are those in the modern world who believe that science and technology provide the answer. Technology, in particular, is universally appealing and pervasive. But technology appeals mostly to human sensations and desires, not to human fulfillment. We can say the same about economics. While the free enterprise system may be a valid form of economic exchange —globally—it hardly serves as a global ethic.

What about establishing a world government? Indeed, a United States of the World! But many of those who have thought about the matter deeply have concluded that such a government would end up as a conglomerate of factious parties and eventually, perhaps, a totalitarian government. The probability of either of these two possibilities forces us to abandon any notion of a world government.

Even so, we can nevertheless envision the possibility of world community, with a common center of shared values and respect for the plurality and diversity of all peoples.

If we define a global ethic as a set of moral principles for determining right and wrong, this must be generally accepted by the peoples of the world. Such a framework must be deeply felt and believed in by the members of the world community.

A global ethic cannot be forced; it must be willingly sought and accepted.

So we can readily understand why religion, science, technology, economics, and a vision of world government cannot serve as the common ethical framework among culturally diverse peoples. Each potential framework is missing something vital. We need a framework that is broader and deeper—one that will capture the hearts and minds of people living in a global environment.

In our quest for a more encompassing framework, a question emerges: What are the criteria for judging the goodness of a common ethical framework for the peoples of the world? How will we know when we have it? The answer is bound to be elusive, but Karl Jaspers, the renowned German philosopher, has provided us with a set of insightful guidelines:

1. The common framework will be allied with the forces truly bent on furthering the destinies and opportunities of all.

2. It must coalesce from what contemporaries see, think, and speak.

3. It will truly be a common framework—a framework for all.

4. It will address the individual, every individual.

5. It will view human persons in terms of their potentialities.

6. It will affirm the essence of human persons in their freedom and their dignity.

7. It will promote the inner freedom of the individual.

8. It will preserve tradition, but adapt it to the needs of the present day.

9. It will build on both the Western and Eastern foundations of humanity.

10. It will foster a humane politics that is attentive to human rights.

11. It will seek simple forms of communication accessible and convincing to everyone.

12. It will not necessarily give us final truths, but will illuminate, direct attention, remove the blinders from our mind's eye.

The essay from which these guidelines were taken is titled "Premises and Possibilities of a New Humanism." In keeping with this title, we can frame the underlying theme of *A Global Ethic* as "the premises and possibilities of a global ethic." What follows is an exploration of these premises and possibilities.

II

THE FRAMEWORK

Since evidence can be adduced and interpreted to corroborate a virtually limitless array of world views, the human challenge is to engage that world view or set of perspectives which brings forth the most valuable, life-enhancing consequences.

RICHARD TARNAS
The Passion of the Western Mind

The search for meaning may very well be our most important quest. But we witness and experience other quests: the quest for security, the quest for love and belonging, the quest for fame and power, and on and on. Underlying all of these is the quest for meaning.

Each human person needs to make sense out of the world: we need to understand how we fit into the total scheme of things. We need to know what significance may be found in our existence. To this end, we need a framework within which to live, a framework that provides meaning and direction.

A well thought out framework should help one answer three fundamental questions: (1) Who am I? (2) What do I believe in? and (3) Where do I stand? These are the basic questions of life, questions that are difficult to answer without the aid of a framework.

Those who have found answers to these questions are likely to experience great satisfaction, because they have purpose and a way, a goal, and a route. Living within a fabric of meaning and significance, they experience fulfillment: "This is what life is all about."

Those many persons who spend much time seeking meaning "out there" may travel to far-away lands attempting to discover meaning. Or they may turn from one guru to another in their search for answers.

These searchers rarely appreciate that the answers lie within themselves. They do not realize that within themselves they have the capability to put meaning into their own lives.

The question is not, "How do I find meaning in life?" but rather, "How do I put meaning into my life?"

THE TEMPLE OF HUMANITY

The quest for meaning requires a framework of moral principles, a framework that can serve both the individual and the global community. Granted that such a framework cannot be definitive or highly prescriptive, it nevertheless can serve as a structure of ideas. As a progressive framework, it can serve as an initial step on an important journey, a never-ending journey.

As an aid in constructing the framework, we will address Immanuel Kant's four fundamental questions: (1) What is man? (2) What can I know? (3) What should I do? and (4) What may I hope for? In focusing on the global community and human relations within this community, we will reword the questions: (1) What does it mean to be human? (2) What can we know? (3) What should we do? and (4) What may we hope for?

These four questions essentially mark off what Karl Jaspers calls "the field of philosophy in its cosmopolitan significance." The question, "What does it mean to be human?" is grounded in philosophical anthropology. The question, "What can we know?" is the topic of epistemology. The question, "What should we do?" is the theme of ethics. And the question, "What may we hope for?" is addressed by metaphysics.

These questions are universal and call for universal answers. If we can arrive at satisfactory answers to these four questions—answers that the global community might agree upon—then we would indeed have a framework for a global ethic.

Where do we turn to find answers to these fundamental questions? The previously mentioned world views—science, religion, philosophy, and daily life—can provide guidance. Will one of these world views provide more acceptable answers than the others? Or even better: How will each world view answer the four questions?

As we construct the framework for a global ethic, we must consider a fifth world view, which is quite different from the other four. Nihilism, which claims that the quest for meaning is for naught, contends that traditional beliefs and values are unfounded and that existence is senseless and useless. With this view being espoused by such a notable personage as Nietzsche, we cannot easily dismiss it. We must at least acknowledge it—as one viewpoint among others.

Now with four positive world views (science, religion, philosophy, and daily life) and one negative world view (nihilism), how do we integrate these five world views into a meaningful framework?

F. Forrester Church, a Unitarian minister, provides us an imaginative metaphor:

> I use an image of a cathedral, which I call the cathedral of the world. It has many, many windows, and we can't even get close to exploring one apse during our lifetime. But we are born in one part of the cathedral, and our parents and grand-parents and neighbors teach us the ways in which to see the light shining through a given window, the one that carries the story of our people, the story of our faith.*

With acknowledgment and thanks to Reverend Church, our metaphor for Humanitas—our framework for a global ethic—will be "The Temple of Humanity." Given that a temple is a place devoted to a special or exalted purpose, what could be more special or exalted than the subject of a common ethic for the global community? The Temple of Humanity is

---

*In *A World of Ideas*, by Bill Moyers.

indeed a magnificent edifice. In addition to the beautiful architecture, it is filled with life—with all the richness of meaning, purpose, and self-fulfillment that puts substance into humanity.

The temple contains six chambers: the atrium, four apses, and a cellar. The atrium is the central chamber of the edifice. Surrounding the four sides of the atrium in semicircle design are the four apses. Directly beneath the atrium is the cellar.

With this image of the temple, we can now assign a place for each of the world views. As shown in the figure, each of the four positive world views—science, religion, philosophy, and

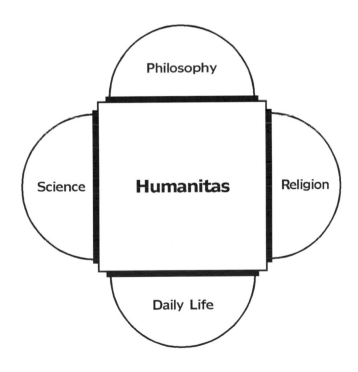

The Temple of Humanity

daily life—is located in an apse. (It is important to note that the four apses are equal in size and prominence.) In the cellar, directly beneath the atrium but not shown in the diagram, is nihilism.

The atrium of the temple represents Humanitas, which is the centerpiece of our framework. The essence of Humanitas, which is the Latin word for humanity, is captured in an essay entitled "Hebrew Humanism" by Martin Buber:

> I am using the word *humanitas* to imply that we are not merely striving for an intellectual movement, but for one which will encompass all of life's reality.

It is here in the atrium, because of the glass dome overarching the temple, that we find the greatest amount of light. Through the glass-stained windows around the perimeter of the temple, a moderate amount of light shines into each apse. But in the cellar, which is below ground level and without windows, we find no light.

Our basic thesis is that each of the six chambers has a rightful place in the Temple of Humanity. Certainly, the atrium is central, without which the edifice would not even be a temple. Removing any of the apses destroys symmetry and completeness. And, yes, even the cellar merits brief occasional visits—for what Karl Jaspers would call a "loosening process."

Our metaphoric temple is a means for integrating and portraying the six world views. The question for each person then becomes: Where is your center of gravity? That is, where is the locus of your innermost being, your internal gyroscope? Is it in one of the four apses? The cellar? Or the atrium?

Residing exclusively or restricting ourselves to any one of the six chambers is counterproductive. Too much time in the cellar, for example, can lead only to cynicism, anguish, and depression. Residing exclusively in any one of the four apses may lead to fanaticism and dogmatism. And even attempting to restrict one's place of residence to the atrium is problematic.

Without the benefit of the four apses, the atrium would not even be an atrium. It would be only a chamber, and a vacuous chamber at that.

Underlying the proposal for a global ethic is the belief that there is a rightful place for all six chambers of the temple. Each of the four apses (science, religion, philosophy, and daily life) extends our horizons and enriches our lives. The cellar (nihilism), even though negative, forces us to examine our underlying assumptions and prevents us from clinging to a single world view, which keeps us calibrated and balanced. And the atrium (Humanitas) provides centering and serves as the common ground for all people of good will to engage in dialogue.

The Germans have a single word for world view: *Weltanschauung*. Literally, it means "manner of looking at the world." What we are proposing here is that Humanitas can become a universal *Weltanschauung*—a common ethic for the global community. It will be an ethic that is open to all.

Given the four basic questions with which we began this essay and the five world views, we can construct a framework for a global ethic. This framework is summarized in the table on the following page. Along the left side of the table are the questions and along the top of the table are the world views. In the cells are the key concepts that connect the questions and the world views. This table is a skeleton outline of the global ethic that is to follow.

DAILY LIFE

Of the four primary world views to be examined—science, religion, philosophy, and daily life—daily life undoubtedly is the closest to reality. This is the world of the concrete, the immediate experience of actual things or events. This is the really real.

THE FRAMEWORK FOR A GLOBAL ETHIC

Basic Questions / World Views	Humanitas	Daily Life	Science	Religion	Philosophy
What Does It Mean to be Human?	The Fully Functioning Person	Coping	Knowing	Believing	Being
What Can We Know?	Wisdom	Experience	Observation	Faith	Reason
What Should We Do?	The Good Life	Contribution	Cooperation*	Compassion	Communication
What May We Hope For?	A Global Community	Rights and Responsibilities	Democracy*	Peace	A Common Ethic

*These two attributes refer to the scientific community rather than to science per se.

The individual who resides exclusively in this apse of the temple spends his or her time dealing with the practical affairs of life. There is no time nor energy to dwell on the abstract, the eloquent, the esthetic, or the ecstatic. The practical matters of the day are all-consuming.

Consider the case of Maria. Here is a woman in her mid-thirties who is the sole provider for herself and her 14-year-old son, Carlos. Her husband left her some ten years ago and she has not seen nor heard from him since.

Maria is one of eight children. Her parents and most of her brothers and sisters live in a nearby village where she and her son spend many of their Sunday afternoons.

Maria has a clerical job in the medical records department of a local hospital. She has mastered the job and performs it well. But her weekly pay barely covers the expenses of the week; nothing is left for savings.

Until recently, Maria spent most of her free time with her son. But now her son has his teen-age friends to hang out with, so Maria is often home alone. She spends her evenings and Saturdays doing the grocery shopping and cleaning the small apartment.

Each week of Maria's life is pretty much the same. Monday through Friday: go to work, come home, fix dinner, wash dishes, encourage Carlos to do his homework, take a bath, go to bed. Saturday: clean the apartment, do the washing, go shopping. Sunday: visit relatives in the nearby village. Then on Monday: start the process all over again.

This scenario pretty well describes Maria's life. It is the world of daily life, and there is not much beyond that. Maria resides in the south apse of the temple and she has little interest in exploring the other apses.

My conversation with Maria confirmed my view that she is very much restricted to the domain of daily life.

When I broached the subject of science, Maria showed little interest. She had taken two years of science in high school, but the courses were taught for rote memory. She recalled receiving reasonably good grades in these courses, but once the final exams were over, she retained very little of the content. The notion of a scientific outlook or attitude had no meaning for Maria.

When I talked with Maria about religion, I found that this world view is not a significant part of her life. Even though she grew up as a Catholic, she now attends church only on special occasions such as weddings and funerals.

When I mentioned philosophy and the life of reason, Maria responded simply with a blank stare. I could have been speaking a foreign language. But after I elaborated on the meaning of reason, she said that it sounded like common sense. And she believed that she was blessed with a great deal of common sense.

In a nutshell, this is Maria's life. It is almost as though she lives in an unchanging cocoon. There is the routine job that she has mastered; there is the apartment to be cleaned and the shopping to be done; there is her 14-year-old son who needs encouragement to complete his homework; there is payday every Friday; there are the family visits on Sunday afternoons; and there is the occasional date on Saturday nights. This is the world of daily life.

Practically all of Maria's time is spent on work, rest, and a little recreation. She tends to the basic needs of life. One might say that this is a life of desire and aversion: seek those things that bring pleasure and avoid those things that cause pain.

Karl Jaspers would say that Maria is restricted to the sphere of empirical existence. And Socrates would note that Maria is a prime example of one who is living the unexamined life.

Maria's life could be likened to a ship without a steering mechanism. The ship keeps moving down the river, but we ask: Where is the steering mechanism that provides the raison d'être?

There is no denying that daily life is an integral part of the whole. It provides us our closest contact with reality. We cannot escape from it, and we should not even try. But if we restrict our lives to this mode of being—and ignore science, religion, and philosophy—our lives will be incomplete.

SCIENCE

Science is so integral to our everyday lives that it is hard to imagine someone going through life with little understanding of its momentous impact. But, for large numbers of people, this is apparently the case.

Science, as one of the four primary world orientations, is important for a number of individuals—especially professional scientists—who find their center of gravity within the west apse of the temple.

Bertrand Russell, in *The Wisdom of the West,* expresses a view that is held by no small number of scientists:

> There are indeed two attitudes that may be adopted toward the unknown. One is to accept the pronouncements of people who say they know, on the basis of books, mysteries, or other sources of inspiration. The other way is to go out and look for oneself, and this is the way of science . . .

The general purpose of science is to understand the natural world. This understanding typically is demonstrated through the grasp of cause-and-effect relationships. If *a*, then *b*.

Aligned with this purpose is the assumption that nature is uniform and predictable. Nature is not capricious.

The essence of science is found not in its content but in its method. We find that the content of the various sciences—physics, chemistry, biology, etc.—is indeed different. But the commonality among all of these scientific disciplines is the scientific method. The empirical method of science is grounded in a four-step process: measuring, relating, predicting, and verifying. And this process is essentially the same for all of the sciences.

The empirical method leads to a high degree of objective certainty. It is no longer your opinion versus my opinion. We look at the facts and then decide. If our opinions are not supported by the facts, then we must reexamine our opinions.

The truth of science is found in its models of reality. These models are not reality *per se* but represent reality. Does the equation or set of equations lead to accurate predictions? The better the fit between the model and reality, the more accurate the predictions.

Science evolves over time. Scientists conduct their research and report their findings in scientific journals. Through a network of scientists conducting research in a given area, we find a mutual sharing of information. The information builds as in a pyramid—from the base up.

We must understand and appreciate the universality of science. Empirical research findings are valid for the entire world—regardless of nationality or language.

We must also appreciate the link between science and technology. Although we witness the marvels of technology every day—from transportation systems to telecommunication systems to entertainment systems—these technological marvels did not "just happen." They are the outgrowth of years of scientific research.

Given this brief review of the salient attributes of science, consider now the case of Miguel. This internationally recognized biologist has found his home in the west apse of the temple. In addition to serving as Miguel's means of livelihood, science serves as his philosophy of life.

Miguel calls his world view Natural Philosophy. It is grounded in science, guided by science, and propelled by science. Miguel is convinced that science is both necessary and sufficient for constructing a meaningful and complete philosophy of life.

Miguel also is convinced that science will eventually produce a "Theory of Everything." That is, everything in the entire Temple of Humanity—as well as that which lies outside the Temple—will someday be explained by science. It is just a matter of time.

Through his beliefs about the omnipotence of science, Miguel sees little need or place for the other world orientations. Daily life is simply a given: for him, it is in his research laboratory. With regard to religion, once the scientific community establishes the Theory of Everything, there will be no need or place for such concepts as God, Allah, or transcendence. With regard to philosophy, Miguel sees no place for ivory-tower speculation about the nature of the universe. The only thing that has cash-value is the generation of precise hypotheses and the rigorous testing of these hypotheses. Any other approach is for naught.

William James, the popular psychologist/philosopher of the early twentieth century, would place Miguel in the category of the "tough-minded" as opposed to the "tender-minded." Science, rigor, and verification are what it is all about. There is no place for poetry.

Assessing Miguel's views from the vantage point of the atrium, we can see that he has transformed science into scientism. As a systematic approach to uncovering truths about the natural world, empirical science deals with the "is." But scientism goes beyond empirical science to include the "ought." Going from the empirical to the normative is a fantastic leap, and whenever science makes this leap, it appears as a quasi-religion. By offering the world ultimate truths regarding the "ought," science attempts to preempt religion.

We must accept the limitations of science. Without diminishing the importance of science, we must realize that science cannot provide us with ultimate goals. Once the goals have been established, however, science can show us how to get there.

Thus, science is incapable of serving as a complete world view or philosophy of life. Science is indeed an essential part of a synoptic world view, but it is only one apse of the temple.

RELIGION

Science and religion are different world orientations. Is there room for both in the Temple of Humanity? We will have to sort it out.

Religion is defined as the individual's relation to the divine, with divine defined as the sacred, the heavenly, the supremely good. Within the various religions, the divine has been called God, Allah, YHWH, Being, transcendence, Ultimate Reality, or the Great Spirit.

In his book *The World's Religions*, Huston Smith identifies and elaborates on seven principal world religions: Hinduism, Buddhism, Confucianism, Taoism, Islam, Judaism, and Christianity. Three of these religions—Judaism, Christianity, and Islam—are monotheistic and four are not.

What an educational experience to study the world's religions! One approach is to focus on the differences between and among the various religions—and there are numerous differences. But a quite different approach is to focus on the similarities. With this latter approach, one thing in particular stands out: the common theme of the world's religions is the quest for—and teaching of—the basic values that define the good life.

As we study the world's religions, we begin to understand how each religion evolved as part of a given culture; we see that religion and culture are closely aligned. When a person who professes a particular religious faith asks himself or herself this question: Why do I profess this particular faith?—the answer very likely lies in the fact that this particular faith was part of the individual's culture and, importantly, the family tradition. If this question would be reflected upon honestly and deeply, we would find greater tolerance among people of different faiths.

We also might find greater tolerance if people around the globe would understand and appreciate the difference between science and religion. These two world views are not contradictory but are complementary.

Whereas science is grounded in observation and facts, religion is grounded in myths and symbols. Myths are legendary stories that contain important messages about life, both good and bad. While the scientific-minded person might scoff at myths, others will see the value of myths in enriching our lives. Myths provide meaning and direction. To Joseph Campbell, mythology was "the song of the universe, the music of the spheres."

Whereas empirical science leads to objective certainty, religion leads to subjective certainty. With objective certainty, we are in a realm that is universally valid—for all of humankind. With subjective certainty, the individual person is in a realm that is true for him or her. Hans Küng, the Catholic theologian, refers to this subjective certainty as "relative absoluteness." That is, it is true for me—and perhaps only me—but it is *indubitably true for me.*

In the book *All Men Are Brothers*, Mahatma Gandhi makes a similar point:

Religions are different roads converging to the same point. What does it matter that we take different roads, so long as we reach the same goal? In reality, there are as many religions as there are individuals.

Whereas science is guided by reason, religion is guided by faith. Some theologians of years past held that faith was supreme and declared war on reason. But Immanuel Kant no doubt was correct when he responded that anyone who declares a war on reason will surely lose. Instead of war, why not collaboration? Inasmuch as the Temple of Humanity has a place for both science and religion, it also has a place for both reason and faith.

Here, then, is someone who has located his center of gravity exclusively within the east apse of the temple. Abdullah is a devout Muslim; his parents, grandparents, and six children are Muslims. In fact, practically everyone in his village is a Muslim.

Abdullah has committed his life to the Islamic faith. He believes that the Divine Word was revealed in Arabic to the Prophet Muhammad in the seventh century. What Allah revealed to the Prophet Muhammad is recorded in the Koran, which Abdullah knows by heart. Abdullah prays five times each day, fasts during the lunar month of Ramadam, and has made the pilgrimage to Mecca. Abdullah does not consume alcohol nor does he eat pork. In essence he has submitted his will to Allah.

By all standards, one would have to agree that Abdullah is a devout Muslim. The rules of life are spelled out in the Koran, and Abdullah lives by these rules. His center of gravity is definitely located in the east apse.

From a synoptic view, there are both positive and negative effects resulting from Abdullah's commitment to the Islamic faith. Let's consider both.

On the positive side, Abdullah's life is indeed focused. It is centered in the Islamic faith and guided by the Koran. This centering provides him with meaning and direction. He is grasped by something that transcends the world of immanence; he lives in the life of the spirit. He is at peace with himself.

On the negative side, Abdullah is convinced that there is only one way to the top of the mountain and that is his way. Having resided in only one small section of the east apse, Abdullah has little knowledge or appreciation of the other religions or other world views. All that he has heard over the years is that anyone who is not a Muslim is a pagan.

We can only conclude that religion has both a beatific side and a shadow side. On the beatific side, we find centeredness, meaning, direction, and an uplifting of the human spirit. On the shadow side, we find intolerance, distrust of those of different faiths, and the sacrifice of reason.

Especially disturbing are the great evils carried out under the guise of religion. All can be attributed to one root problem: those isolated within a particular world view are completely unaware of the shadow side of their faith. These people don't know that they don't know.

Even so, there is a definite place for religion in the Temple of Humanity. This world view deserves an apse of its own and one that is equal in size and prominence to the other three apses. But the temple will be selective in choosing religions of a certain type: that will lift people up rather than take them down, that will broaden people rather than shrink them, one that will help followers become fully functioning persons.

Placed over the entrance to the east apse of the temple are these words of wisdom by Mahatma Gandhi: "The messenger of peace must have equal regard for all of the principal religions of the earth." The Temple of Humanity needs many messengers of peace.

PHILOSOPHY

In the north apse of the temple we explore the fourth world view: philosophy. Many think philosophy is simply a college course taken to satisfy a humanities requirement. But philosophy is much more—at least it has the potential to be much more.

In times past, philosophy was considered to be a principal world view, a world orientation, a way of life, especially by the troika of early Greek philosophers—Socrates, Plato, and Aristotle. Later philosophers—Plotinus, Spinoza, Hume, Kant, Bruno, Leibniz, Hegel, Whitehead, Jaspers, and others—considered philosophy to be their "way of life."

Philosophy as a world orientation is more difficult to define than either science or religion. The meaning of philosophy has changed over the centuries and, even today, it means different things to different people—including the professional philosophers themselves.

To the early Greek philosophers, philosophy was the love of wisdom . . . and wisdom was much more than the mere possession of information.

Karl Jaspers, in *Way to Wisdom*, makes special note of the roots of the word "philosophy":

> The Greek word for philosopher (*philosophos*) connotes a distinction from sophos. It signifies the lover of wisdom (knowledge) as distinguished from him who considers himself wise in the possession of knowledge.

Some would define philosophy as the life of reason. With science being the life of observation and facts and religion being the life of faith, philosophy is set apart by being the life of reason. By using our rational powers we will find our way.

Others would define philosophy as the search for truth. Linking reason and truth, one might say that these are two sides of the same coin. The philosopher seeks truth via reason.

Philosophy means to be on the way, searching for truth through reason, on a never-ending journey. As specific questions are answered, new questions emerge. And so the process continues.

Philosophy attempts to clarify the whole. Many professional persons are specialists who learn more and more about less and less. But philosophers counter this trend by cutting across specific disciplines and specialties to ask the broader questions and seek the broader answers. True philosophers are systems thinkers *par excellence*. They have discarded the separator walls in their memory banks.

True philosophers have become masters of their own thoughts. They accept no position blindly. They listen attentively to various points of view, reflect on them, and then make up their own minds. For a true philosopher, discipleship is out of the question, because addiction to a single individual will stunt one's intellectual development.

Our example here is an individual who has found his center of gravity in the north apse of the temple. Friedrich is a philosophy professor in a major university. He specializes in the philosophy of language and is well known from his numerous publications on the subject.

We asked him what is the purpose of philosophy. And he responded that the principal aim of philosophy is the elimination of nonsense and the clarification of thought.

We asked why philosophy had changed its course from the time of the early Greek philosophers. Some two millennia ago, philosophy had a very broad scope—namely, the understanding of and quest for the good life. Today, however, philosophy—at least in academic circles—is a highly specialized field concentrating primarily on clarifying language.

Friedrich acknowledged that this observation is correct, and he explained that, for philosophy to be on equal footing with science and to hold a position of strength in the university, it must specialize and make a contribution of substance that provides useful tools to the scientist.

As Friedrich responded to the questions, it was evident that he truly lives his philosophy. His life of reason is very narrow. Reason, logic, and clarity pervade his entire being. I could sense logic and precision in his words, his intonations, and even his body language.

After spending the afternoon in Friedrich's office, we drove to his home for dinner. When the evening meal was completed, we relaxed in his family room by the fireplace.

For entertainment, we spent the next two hours discussing puzzles and paradoxes. The Paradox of the Heap is his favorite. It goes like this:

> One grain of sand is not a heap of sand. If something is not a heap of sand, addition (or diminution) by one grain will not make it a heap. But, then, nothing is a heap. For, by starting with one grain of sand and adding to it a grain at a time, we will never have a heap. If something arrived at by such a method is not a heap, then nothing just like it, arrived at by some other method, is a heap either. So there are no heaps of sand and the whole idea is incoherent.*

The following day I reflected on my visit with the world-renowned philosopher. What troubled me most was how philosophy had lost its way. Over the centuries since the early Greek philosophers, philosophy evolved from a way of life to a study of puzzles and paradoxes.

Albert Schweitzer had this to say about philosophy:

> Of gold coinage, minted in the past, philosophy had abundance; hypotheses about a soon to be developed world view filled her vaults like unminted bullion; but food with which to appease the spiritual hunger of the present she did not possess.

---

*In *Introduction to Philosophy*, edited by John Perry and Michael Bratman.

Although disheartened by the meeting with Friedrich, I was heartened by the thought that we laypersons do not have to go the way of the present-day academic philosophers. We can still study the great philosophers of ages past and find our way through them.

As for philosophy in the Temple of Humanity, it should be one apse of the temple; but it by no means can constitute the total temple. Philosophy has a rightful place alongside science, religion, and daily life—but it cannot go it alone.

HUMANITAS

After exploring the four apses of the Temple of Humanity, let's regain our perspective by examining the temple as a whole. And we need to examine carefully the heart of the temple—the atrium.

Again, consider Martin Buber's framing of the word *humanitas*:

> I am using the word *humanitas* to imply that we are not merely striving for an intellectual movement, but for one which will encompass all of life's reality.

The Latin meaning of *humanitas* is "human nature or character." The Latin roots of the word denote (1) the quality distinguishing civilized people from savages and beasts and (2) humane character, kindness, human feeling. Assume that "humanity" focuses on what humankind *is* and "humanitas" focuses on what humankind *can become*—in a very positive sense.

Thus, the aim of Humanitas is *human flourishing*. The Latin for flourish is *florere*, formed on the root *flor* for flower. Thus, the meaning of flourish is to bloom, to thrive, to prosper, to be fully developed—i.e., to become fully human.

On a global scale, this aim of human flourishing can best be achieved by building a global community, which must be undergirded by a global ethic. This is the essence of the Humanitas philosophy.

As a comprehensive world view or universal *Weltanschauung*, Humanitas is represented by the entire Temple of Humanity. Centered in the atrium, fulfillment is achieved in the four apses. Humanitas embraces all four of the primary world views and integrates them into a real unity.

As stated previously, the Temple of Humanity contains six chambers: four apses, a cellar, and an atrium. The four apses represent the four primary world views: science, religion, philosophy, and daily life. The cellar represents nihilism. And the atrium represents the center of Humanitas. Each chamber makes a significant contribution to the whole.

We have discussed the four primary world views. Each of these world views makes a significant contribution to humanity. Daily life is our compact with reality, as manifested in the everyday world. Science provides us knowledge of the natural world and the foundation for technology. Religion provides us ultimate values and direction. And philosophy provides us the tools of reason. Each is essential for a comprehensive world view; none may be omitted.

Only when one believes that an apse is the atrium do we have distortions. The playing field then becomes slanted, as was the case with Maria, Miguel, Abdullah, and Friedrich. Each was locked into a given apse and thought the apse was the atrium. Being unwilling or unable to venture outside their particular apses, how would they know?

To be at home in the total temple, one need not be an expert in each world view. Being a generalist will be quite adequate. But, to fully appreciate the beauty and depth of daily life, one needs to have experienced both the joys and the sorrows of daily life. To truly understand the other three apses, one needs to be a dedicated student—a searcher, a lifelong learner. Reading and reflecting on selected books in the areas of science, religion, and philosophy offer an appreciation of how important each world view is in the Temple of Humanity. In the study of science, pay special attention to the scientific method. In the study of religion, focus on learning the nature of religion, experiencing one's own religion, and appreciating the world's religions. And in the study of philosophy, focus on the lives and thoughts of the great philosophers and on the basic questions of philosophy. By acquiring a breadth of knowledge and applying it in daily life, one can gradually find self-realization in the atrium of the temple.

And don't forget the cellar, which is home to the nihilists. With a lantern in hand, we should visit the lower chamber occasionally. A brief discussion with Nietzsche will unmask all shams and help keep us honest. But we should not tarry too long, lest we be unduly influenced by the cynics. (Why would an individual forsake the purity of the air in the upper chambers for a dark, damp cellar, and choose it as a permanent residence? Maybe these individuals grew up in one of the four apses and then became disillusioned, disenchanted, and fled through a large crack in the floor—ending up in the cellar.)

Directly above the cellar is the atrium, the central chamber of the temple. The atrium stands in sharp contrast to the cellar: instead of isolation there is involvement; instead of pessimism there is optimism; instead of tearing down there is building up; instead of retreating there is advancing; instead of darkness there is light. We need to examine the atrium more closely.

Residing in the temple's atrium requires an understanding of three levels of learning. First-order learning means that the individual has mastered one particular paradigm (say, Christianity or analytic philosophy) and resides exclusively within that paradigm. Second-order learning occurs when the individual realizes that there is a genuine choice between paradigms (say, between Hinduism and Buddhism). And third-order learning comes about when the individual has a real grasp of paradigms. Residing in the atrium requires a mastery of third-order learning.

Once we reach the atrium, we achieve freedom of thought. The peoples of the world desire many freedoms: freedom of religion, freedom of speech, freedom of the press, and on and on. But what about freedom of thought? We are granted this freedom in the atrium.

The atrium represents the commons for all of humanity. But, realistically, how many people can venture outside their cherished apse and join others in the atrium for dialogue? Very few. Can we expect leaders in the world community to join other leaders in the atrium? Definitely, yes. They have done it in the past, and they are doing it at this very hour.

The challenge for these leaders is to encourage others to at least make an occasional visit to the atrium. And when they make this visit, it is essential that they suspend their assumptions and generalizations, that they be willing to temporarily "put on hold" their preconceived notions in a quest for broader understanding. If this occurs on a large scale, then we would indeed have made a giant step toward the overarching aim of Humanitas: enhancement of human flourishing by building a global community.

Given this introduction to Humanitas, we can now address four fundamental questions: (1) What does it mean to be human? (2) What can we know? (3) What should we do? and (4) What may we hope for? These questions will be answered in the light of the Temple of Humanity.

III

THE FULLY FUNCTIONING PERSON

The process of becoming a leader is much the same as the process of becoming an integrated human being. For the leader, as for an integrated person, life itself is the career. Discussing the process in terms of "leaders" is merely a way of making it concrete.

WARREN BENNIS
On Becoming a Leader

We now address the first of the four fundamental questions: What does it mean to be human? Have you ever asked yourself the question, What do I need to do to become a fully integrated person—one who "has it all together"? This question is basic to one's self-development. As a point of departure, let's listen to a hypothetical dialogue between Socrates and Lysis.

Socrates was going from the Academy straight to the Lyceum, intending to take the outer road, which is close by the wall to the city. When he came to the rear gate of the city, which is by the fountain of Panops, he fell in with Lysis, the eldest son of Democrates, and a company of young men who were standing with him. Lysis, seeing Socrates approach, asked where he was going.

Socrates: I am going from the Academy straight to the Lyceum.

Lysis: Then come straight to us and put in here; we need your counsel.

Socrates: Who are your friends?

Lysis: I believe that you know each one of them: Laches, Charmides, and Nicias.

Socrates: Indeed, I do know each one of you and I know your families. But I ask, Lysis, why do you need my counsel?

Lysis: Socrates, for most of the day, the four of us have been discussing a very heavy question. We seem to be on the right track, but we are not certain.

36

Socrates: And what is the question?

Lysis: Well, first, I will give you a little background. It started when Nicias referred to a certain individual, who will remain unnamed, as being very inhuman. And all of us agreed that this individual is inhuman. I then posed this question to the group: If we know what it means to be *inhuman*, do we know what it means to be *human*? And that became our question: What does it mean to be human?

Laches: We then altered the question somewhat to this: What is a fully functioning person?

Lysis: That is correct. And all of us agreed that it is better to be a fully functioning person than a partially functioning person. We also agreed that the individual we were referring to previously is only a partially functioning person.

Socrates: Well, I certainly agree, Lysis, the four of you are addressing a very heavy question. And I would like to ask you this: Are you attempting to define a fully functioning person just for Athens or for a broader region?

Lysis: We would think the latter, Socrates. We believe that a model of the fully functioning person that is relevant for Athens would be just as relevant for Sparta or for any other city-state in the world.

Socrates: I see. Well, tell me, where are you in the quest?

Lysis: Something that we have learned from you is that the fully functioning person is a good person, a virtuous person. Such a person does not lie, cheat, or steal.

Socrates: I understand what you are saying. But what about the man who is drowned in drink all day long. I know such a man; he sits in a stupor most of the day. And I can state with considerable confidence that he does not lie, cheat, or steal. Would you say that this man is a fully functioning person?

Lysis: Indeed not, Socrates. We also agreed that the fully functioning person is a temperate person. He is moderate in all of his actions. So the man you describe would not meet this requirement.

Socrates: Are you saying that anything that one does is acceptable, so long as it is done in moderation?

Lysis: I believe so.

Socrates: But what about lying, cheating, and stealing? Is it acceptable to do these things—so long as they are done in moderation?

Lysis: No, not at all. It seems that some things are off limits. There are some things that are simply wrong in and of themselves. Another example would be adultery. The notion of temperance simply does not apply to such things.

Socrates: Well stated, Lysis. But I am searching for the central thread. The question we are addressing is, What is a fully functioning person? What does it mean to be fully human? You have mentioned two attributes of the fully functioning person—being good and being temperate. But what is the *essence* of being a fully functioning person?

Lysis: We also agreed that love and friendship are essential attributes. The fully functioning person has loving relations with others and is able to make and keep friendships alive.

Socrates: I must agree with you. And as I look at the four of you, I think how important friendship is. But I am still searching for the *essence*.

Lysis: We also agreed that the fully functioning person is a courageous person. And I believe that we are able to distinguish between being courageous and being foolhardy.

Socrates: It is commendable that you can make this distinction. But I still come back to my basic question: What is the *essence* of being a fully functioning person?

Lysis: Well, we agreed that the fully functioning person is one who lives a life of reason. He is dedicated to a search for truth through reason and is able to control his passions through his rational powers.

Socrates: I certainly must agree with you, Lysis, about the importance of a life of reason, but I fail to see that this gets at the essence of what it means to be a fully functioning person.

Lysis: Well, what about wisdom? We agreed that wisdom is broader than reason.

Socrates: How do you mean? Can you explain?

Lysis: We believe that reason refers to intellectual powers only. But wisdom is much more. We believe that wisdom is reason plus compassion. And we believe that this view of wisdom applies to you, Socrates.

Socrates: I am honored that you view me that way. But you still have failed to answer my basic question: What is the *essence* of being a fully functioning person? You have listed a number of important attributes: virtue, temperance, love and friendship, courage, reason, and wisdom. And I commend you and your friends for arriving at this remarkable list of attributes. I agree with each one of them. But the important thing to appreciate is that they are attributes, not the essence. So my question remains: What is the *essence* of being a fully functioning person?

Lysis: Socrates, can you give me an example?

Socrates: Do you recall the time that you, Charmides, and I were discussing the nature of democracy?

Lysis: Indeed I do. That was a most stimulating discussion.

Socrates: Well, you may recall that we began by listing some of the features of a democratic state, such as the right to vote and trial by jury.

Lysis: I recall that very clearly.

Socrates: Well, the breakthrough in our discussion came about when we agreed that the essence of democracy is government by the people. We can define democracy as government by the people; this is the essence, the heart of the matter. The right to vote and trial by jury are simply features of democracy.

Lysis: I understand what you are saying.

Socrates: In a similar way, I am seeking the essence of what it means to be a fully functioning person. I am reminded of the comedy in which it was stressed, "How delightful a thing a human being could be, if he were a human being." And that is what we are now discussing: What it means to be a human being.

Lysis: Socrates, I beg your forgiveness. I trust that you do not take me for being dim-witted, but I believe that I now understand your question.

Socrates: Indeed not, Lysis. I hope that I have not even suggested that you are dim-witted. You are one of my most prized students. And I hope that my questions do not come across as being an attack on your good judgment, for I am also asking myself this question: What is the essence of being a fully functioning person? I have not framed a satisfactory answer in my own mind.

Lysis: I believe I have an answer to your question. I believe that I have a reasonable answer.

Socrates: Please tell me. I would like to know the answer. And I am certain that your friends, Laches, Charmides, and Nicias, also would like to know your answer to the question.

Lysis: I will frame the answer in this manner: The fully functioning person is one who has mastered the art of living. By "living," I mean all of living, and living is an art. The fully functioning person is one who has mastered this art. In essence, the fully functioning person is one who has achieved personal mastery in the art of living.

Socrates: You monster! By the dog! You have been leading me round in a circle. Have you known this answer all along?

Lysis: No, truly not, Socrates. I arrived at this conclusion only through your relentless questioning and your helping me understand the difference between attribute and essence. I am grateful to you now just as I have been in the past and expect to be in the future. You have helped me get to the heart of the matter. My friends and I thank you.

Socrates: And I thank you for allowing me to be part of this dialogue. It has been a learning experience for me. I hope that in our next meeting we will be able to explore the question, What is the art of living? But that must wait, because now I must bid you farewell and continue my journey to the Lyceum.

THE TEMPLE OF HUMAN POTENTIAL

Lysis has captured the essence of what it means to be a fully functioning person: to master the art of living. Thus the next logical question is: What does it mean to master the art of living?

An unknown author provides a context:

Many men know the laws of mathematics and are skilled in the arts, but most men know very little about the laws governing life, the art of living. One may be able to build an airplane and circle the globe and yet be entirely ignorant of the simple art of how to be happy, successful, and content. When studying the arts, place first upon the list the *art of living.*

A framework for the art of living is provided by the Temple of Humanity. As you will recall, this temple has six chambers: four apses, a cellar, and an atrium. The four apses represent the common world views: daily life, science, religion, and philosophy; the cellar represents nihilism; and the atrium represents the universal *Weltanschauung*—Humanitas.

The mirror of the Temple of Humanity is the Temple of Human Potential, which is shown on the following page. Forgetting the cellar, these are the corresponding chambers:

- Humanitas: the Art of Living
- Daily Life: the Art of Coping
- Science: the Art of Knowing
- Religion: the Art of Believing
- Philosophy: the Art of Being

To aid our understanding, we must define each chamber:

- The Art of Living: good judgment, discernment
- The Art of Coping: contending in the everyday world with some degree of success
- The Art of Knowing: acquiring objective knowledge from the world at large
- The Art of Believing: being committed to and living by a set of core values
- The Art of Being: achieving selfhood, being a unique and authentic person

Given these definitions, our basic premise is that the fully functioning person lives out of the total temple. All four apses

42

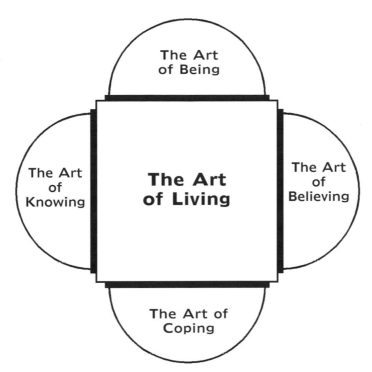

The Temple of Human Potential

are essential for a fully functioning life, and the atrium serves as the center of gravity. Neglecting any one of the five chambers prevents one from becoming a fully functioning person.

A corollary to this premise is that each human being is born with the potential to live out of the total temple, regardless of place of birth, education, economics, or any other factor.

Focusing on human potential is ideal for our quest for a global ethic. Directing our attention only to human actuality highlights the vast differences among the world's people. But directing our attention to human potential allows us to discover what the people of the globe have in common. We may indeed find that there is a common human nature—a universal human nature—found in human potential.

In *Truth in Religion*, Mortimer Adler puts it this way:

> In what sense then is there a human nature, a specific nature that is common to all members of the species? The answer can be given in a single word: potentialities. Human nature is constituted by all the potentialities that are the species-specific properties common to all members of the human species.

What we need in our quest is a universal model of human potential—one that will apply to humankind at large. And this is the intent of the Temple of Human Potential.

Let's now examine each of the five chambers of this temple, beginning with the atrium, the Art of Living.

THE ART OF LIVING

If we closely observe people who seem to have mastered the art of living, we find that they differ from one another in many ways, and each is a unique human being. But one attribute they have in common is *good judgment*, especially in their ability to discern the desirable from the undesirable.

Consider the following examples. For each of the 20 pairs that follow, the *first* is a trait of a person who has mastered the art of living and the *second* is the extreme of the first trait, sort of an out-of-control version.

Centered vs. Self-Centered* A centered person is guided by an internal gyroscope, a moral compass, which provides unity and direction. The self-centered person believes that the world

---

*Most of the definitions that follow are taken from *The Random House Dictionary of the English Language*.

revolves around his or her own being, that the world exists to serve his or her own selfish interests.

Good vs. Sanctimonious A good person lives a life of virtue and of moral excellence. A sanctimonious person makes a showy display of religious devotion or righteousness.

Generous vs. Extravagant A generous person is liberal in giving, as well as unstinting and unselfish. The extravagant person is wasteful, and goes beyond what is deserved or justifiable.

Interested vs. Meddlesome An interested person is sincerely engaged and has a genuine interest in another's well-being. The meddlesome person involves himself or herself in a matter without right or invitation.

Tolerant vs. Indifferent The tolerant person holds a fair and objective attitude toward opinions and practices that differ from his or her own. The indifferent person is without interest or concern, is not caring.

Open-Minded vs. Wishy-Washy The open-minded person has a mind receptive to new ideas or arguments, is unprejudicial. The wishy-washy person is lacking in decisiveness, is without strength of character.

Acquiescent vs. Docile The acquiescent person assents tacitly, complies. The docile person is malleable, is easily managed or handled.

Assertive vs. Aggressive The assertive person has the ability and willingness to defend one's claims or rights. The aggressive person initiates unprovoked attacks on the other.

Self-Confident vs. Arrogant The self-confident person has a realistic and objective confidence in his or her own judgment or ability. The arrogant person makes unwarrantable claims or pretensions to superior importance or rights, exhibits assumed or real superiority.

Trusting vs. Gullible The trusting person relies on the integrity of others, is confident in his or her expectations. The gullible person is easily deceived or cheated.

Candid vs. Cruel The candid person is straightforward, open, and sincere. The cruel person willfully or knowingly causes pain or distress to others, and enjoys the pain or distress of others.

Cooperative vs. Servile The cooperative person works or acts with others willingly for a common purpose or benefit. The servile person is slavishly submissive or obsequious, fawning.

Rational vs. Heartless The rational person exercises reason or sound judgment, is endowed with the faculty of reason. The heartless person is unfeeling, unkind, unsympathetic.

Courageous vs. Foolhardy The courageous person has the quality of mind or spirit that enables him or her to face difficulty or danger with firmness. The foolhardy person is bold without judgment, is foolishly rash or reckless.

Knowledgeable vs. Ostentatious The knowledgeable person possesses knowledge, insight, or understanding, is well-informed and discerning. The ostentatious person is characterized by pretentious show, a display intended to impress others.

Expressive vs. Loquacious The expressive person is able to convey a thought, an attitude of mind, or emotion in an effective or vivid manner. The loquacious person is characterized by a disposition toward excessive talk, to be chattering or babbling.

Persuasive vs. Manipulative The persuasive person induces change through rational argument. The manipulative person induces change through unfair or seductive means.

Humorous vs. Crass The humorous person displays a genuine sense of fun and the comic. The crass person lacks refinement or sensitivity, is gross or obtuse.

Imaginative vs. Foolish The imaginative person demonstrates the ability to meet and resolve difficulties resourcefully. The foolish person displays lack of common sense or good judgment, is unwise.

Unique vs. Odd The unique person is one of a kind, special. The odd person is singular or peculiar in a freakish or eccentric way.

In these twenty pairs of terms, the ones on the left characterize the person who has mastered the art of living. Those on the right characterize the person who has not mastered the art of living. And most important: the person who has mastered the art of living profoundly understands and can discern the differences between the terms on the left and those on the right. How to be discerning cannot be found in a rule book; it comes about through practice in the art of living.

With the art of living being represented by the atrium of the Temple of Human Potential, we now move to the apses. Here there are four extensions to the art of living: the art of coping, the art of knowing, the art of believing, and the art of being.

THE ART OF COPING

The art of coping is the ability to contend in the everyday world with some degree of success. In *No Easy Victories*, John Gardner states it well:

> Life never was a series of easy victories (not even a series of hard victories). We cannot win every round or arrive at a neat solution to every problem. But driving, creative effort to solve problems is the breath of life, for a civilization or an individual.

Some people might disagree with Gardner. Mayla is a case in point. Mayla had been a happy wife and mother. She had a kind, considerate husband who took care of her and protected her. But that was the problem: he over-protected her. By taking complete responsibility for all household and financial matters, Mayla's husband actually did her a disservice: he stole her self-hood (and she let it go). When he died unexpectedly, he left his wife in a quandary. Finding herself alone with three children and numerous household and financial responsibilities, Mayla did not know which way to turn. Lamenting on Mayla's plight, her sister remarked, "Mayla is unable to cope."

On the positive side, there are others who truly know how to cope. Otto is an excellent case in point. This scientist-manager took over the management of a research laboratory that was plagued with numerous problems: funding was rapidly declining because of dissatisfied clients, facilities and equipment were becoming obsolete, and staff morale, as would be expected, was low. Otto saw the job as a challenge. By meeting with clients to discuss their concerns, by developing a facilities and equipment renewal plan, by implementing a comprehensive staff development program, and by taking a number of other constructive measures, Otto was able to turn the laboratory around in a little more than a year. One of Otto's staff members remarked, "Our director is a person who knows how to cope."

The fully functioning person knows how to cope. What is the art of coping? We offer the following guidelines.

Problem Solving

We humans are faced with problems throughout our lives. Some problems are momentous and some are trivial. Regardless of the magnitude or the context, a problem exists when there is some type of barrier or obstacle between us and the goal. We must find a way around, over, or under the barrier. And sometimes we might be able to remove the barrier. This is the essence of problem solving.

To master the art of coping, we must master the art of problem solving. And we can learn this art.

In *The Art of Problem Solving*, Edward Hodnett puts it this way:

> Learning to solve problems is like learning to play baseball. You learn to throw, to catch, to bat, to run bases, to make plays, and to execute all sorts of refinements of these basic skills. You do not learn to play baseball. You learn these basic skills separately, and you put them together in new combinations in every game.

Viewing Problems as Opportunities

It is so tempting to ignore problems. The ostrich dynamic is more attractive than coping. We are threatened by problems; they simply overwhelm us. Happiness would be a life without problems! Unfortunately, this reluctance to cope only exacerbates the problem. Most problems will not "fade away"; they must be confronted.

But a life without problems would also be very boring. If we could choose to live a life completely devoid of problems— even small problems—how many would choose such a life? Probably not very many, simply because there would be no challenges. Thus, rather than viewing problems as threats or something that should be avoided, we can view them as opportunities—to test our mettle and to learn and to grow. Such an attitude can transform a threatening situation into a challenging situation, from "problem" to "opportunity."

Being a Doer Rather Than a Victim

When confronted with problems, it is so easy to fall into the Victim mode. Shifting the blame to other individuals or to "the system" lets the Victim "off the hook."

With regard to responsibility and accountability, the Victim and the Doer stand at polar opposites. The Victim whines and complains; the Doer copes. The Victim bemoans constraints; the Doer learns to function effectively within the constraints. The Victim spends a great deal of time commiserating with other Victims; the Doer spends time dealing with the problems.

The Victim mode leads to at least three undesirable consequences. First, the individual who typically assumes this role is not very productive, because so much energy is consumed in whining, blaming, and commiserating. Second, Victims tend to bring their associates down—both in their performance and in their outlooks on life. And third, perennial Victims will never become fully functioning persons, because their negativism thwarts their growth.

Each person has a choice: To be a Victim or to be a Doer. Why not choose the latter?

Understanding the Environment

Every problem must be solved within a given environment. The environment may be your home, your place of work, the volunteer agency where you spend time, or a governmental agency from which you are seeking some type of service.

Every environment is different. Consequently, a problem solving approach that might have been highly effective in one particular environment might be a complete failure in another. And you might find yourself dismayed and puzzled by the failure.

Take time to learn the culture of any organization with which you plan to spend a significant amount of time. Culture is defined as "how we do things around here." Culture isn't in the operational handbook. You learn the organizational culture only by observing carefully and asking lots of questions.

By learning that culture, you can get things done effectively and efficiently. You can cope.

Defining the Problem

Whenever faced with a problem, some people want to move quickly to a solution. Never mind that we have not actually defined the problem at hand; just come up with a solution so we can move on to the next one. This is typical for action-oriented people.

The saying, "A problem clearly defined is half-solved," is astute. With a poorly defined problem, we hardly know which way to turn. But with a clearly defined problem, a reasonable course of action is easier to find.

So before you move on to subsequent steps in the problem solving process, be sure that you have clearly defined the problem. Keep asking "Why?" Once an initial problem statement has been proposed, ask "Why?" When an answer has been offered, ask another "Why?" Continue asking "Why?" until you believe that you have arrived at the root cause of the problem. Through this process, you will likely attack the *real* problem rather than its symptoms.

Starting With the End in Mind

The typical approach to solving a problem starts with where we are now. We focus on whatever is immediately in front of us: a barrier to overcome or something to be fixed. Concrete realities have a way of grasping our attention, of making us focus. This approach, however, tends to focus on the problem, not the solution. And we really do not know where we might end up.

A better approach is to start with the end in mind. This is one of the fundamental principles recommended by Harold Geneen, former chief executive officer of a large corporation, on how to run a business. In his autobiography, *Geneen*, the author offers a Three-Sentence Course on Business Management: "You read a book from the beginning to the end. You run a business the opposite way. You start with the end, and then you do everything you must to reach it."

Whether solving a specific problem or running a business (which involves solving innumerable problems), start with the end in mind. After you have clearly defined the problem, describe the situation if the problem-solving effort is successful. *Then work back from that end state*. This approach can likely heighten your problem solving ability.

The Courage to Confront

Many situations that call for effective coping involve people, other human beings. When the barrier standing between us and our goal is one or more individuals, how do we deal with it?

Very few people have both the skill and the willingness to confront others who are creating problems for them. It's so difficult to confront others who create problems for us. Is it because we think we need to be loved by everyone? Is it because we do not want to hurt the other person's feelings? Is it because we dislike the tension created by confrontation? Perhaps it is a mix of all of these.

When others do create problems for us, we can respond in any one of three ways: avoid, attack, or confront. Individuals who are proficient in coping neither avoid nor attack the individual who might be causing the problem. Rather, they confront the individual in a straightforward manner. Importantly, *they set upon the problem rather than the person*.

During a wedding ceremony, the officiating priest said to the young couple that he wanted to offer them just one piece of advice for achieving and maintaining a successful marriage: "Before you go to sleep at night, be sure that you have resolved the interpersonal issues of the day. Tomorrow you will be faced with new problems, and you do not want to carry the old problems over to the next day." That was sound advice.

Being Assertive Rather Than Aggressive

There is a fine line between being assertive and being aggressive. But it is an important distinction.

Consider the salient differences between the two approaches. When you assert yourself, you are declaring and affirming; when you are aggressive, you are pushing and attacking. When you assert yourself, you are stating strongly and positively your position on a given issue; when you are aggressive, you are launching a vigorous and menacing attack against others. The discerning person sees a world of difference between the two approaches.

In deciding which approach to employ in a given situation, consider the likely consequences. By being aggressive, by attacking the other, you very likely will find yourself in a win-lose relationship. But by being assertive, you can end with a win-win relationship.

The person who is proficient in coping chooses assertiveness rather than aggressiveness, because it promises greater long-term success.

Thinking Win-Win

In a conflict situation, we can hold either of two attitudes: win-lose or win-win. There is considerable difference between these two attitudes.

Watching sports events tends to condition us to think win-lose. In every basketball game, for example, there will be a winner and a loser. If the score is tied at the end of the game, then the two teams will go into an overtime period. And if the score is still tied at the end of the first overtime period, there will be a second overtime period, and so on until one team is the outright victor.

This win-lose attitude carries over into our everyday lives. What if two people want access to the same resource on the same day? This resource might be a physical facility, a piece of equipment, or a human helper. If two parties assume at the outset that only one party can have access to the resource on this particular day, there will be a winner and a loser.

With a win-win attitude, in a conflict situation, the question becomes: How can we both win in this situation? Can I use the resource in the morning, and you could use it in the afternoon? Or perhaps can I have access to it on Tuesday, and you on Wednesday? This merely requires a little creative thinking—done in the spirit of collaboration.

For the person proficient in coping, win-win becomes a way of life.

Perseverance

Most of us will face failure sometime in our lives. This may be a failure in seeking political office, in a business enterprise, or even in a marriage. The issue is not so much whether or not we have suffered failures, but how we recovered from them. The basic question is whether or not we can cope.

A supreme example of the ability to cope was demonstrated by Abraham Lincoln, the sixteenth President of the United States. This was Lincoln's road to the White House:

- Failed in business in 1831
- Defeated for Legislature in 1832
- Failed in business in 1833
- Suffered nervous breakdown in 1836
- Defeated for Speaker in 1838
- Defeated for Elector in 1840

- Defeated for Congress in 1843
- Defeated for Congress in 1848
- Defeated for Senate in 1855
- Defeated for Vice President in 1856
- Defeated for Senate in 1858
- Elected President in 1860.

* * *

These guidelines elucidate the Coping mode. They are by no means all-inclusive, but they might point the way.

If we look at the Coping mode in its totality, within the context of the Temple of Human Potential, what if a given individual lives essentially in the Coping mode and is oblivious to the other three modes? This individual would lack basic knowledge, core values, and an internal gyroscope for decision making. The result would be a myopic individual, one whose vision was seriously impaired. At best, we would have only a partially functioning human being. Only in conjunction with the other three modes can the Coping mode be truly manifested.

THE ART OF KNOWING

Confucius, that wise Chinese philosopher, understood the nature of "profound knowledge":

Confucius said, "Ah, Sze, do you suppose that I merely learned a great deal and tried to remember it all?" "Yes, isn't that what you do?" "No," said Confucius, "I have a system or a central thread that runs through it all."

Twenty-five hundred years after Confucius we find ourselves in an information age. We are bombarded daily with all sorts of information, some of which we want and some we don't. Many people complain of an information overload. One thing we know for certain: We cannot advance by simply taking in more and more information and storing it in our memories. There must be a better way.

The fully functioning person has found a better way: mastering the art of learning. Salient features of this art are presented below.

A Commitment to Lifelong Learning

Upon completion of high school, many of us attended what was called a "graduation" ceremony. The speaker for the occasion would present an inspirational message and wish the new graduates success in life. Each of the new graduates would then be handed a diploma that signified successful completion of the course of study.

I have often thought that "graduation" was a poor choice of words, because it signifies "completion." And certainly no high school graduate or even college graduate should assume that he or she has *completed* a course of study. This is only the bare beginning.

Commencement, a seemingly interchangeable term for graduation, is a far better name for the event. Again, the speaker delivers an inspirational message. Now the theme of the program more correctly is "a beginning." The message to the students is: you are ready to *begin* learning. The formal academic program has provided basic knowledge and basic tools for learning, and the journey begins.

Each of us should make a commitment to lifelong learning. We should be active learners for the rest of our lives. Even as we age, there is no biological reason to stop learning. It is simply a matter of will.

Taking Charge of Your Own Learning

Unfortunately, high school and college did not prepare us very well to take charge of our own learning. For some twelve, sixteen, or even twenty years, our learning was prescribed. For the most part, the assignments were given by teachers, instructors, and professors, and as students, we dutifully completed the assignments.

Carrying the same paradigm to the world of work, we might find job training programs laid out in a logical sequence. To advance our careers, we should complete both the required and the optional courses.

In either academia or on-the-job training, these approaches are okay, except we become overly conditioned to assume that some external agent will decide what, when, and how we will learn. So we passively await the announcement of the next course offering.

It is important—and even essential—to shift from recipient of learning to director of learning. Take charge of your own learning: direct your own learning, because you should know better than anyone else exactly what new learning you need and when you need it. Seek counsel from others, but take charge.

Learning How to Learn

Learning involves both content and process. But in formal education, most of the emphasis was placed on content, with relatively little emphasis on process. The focus was on "what" we learn rather than "how" we learn. Then, in our adult years, we discover that much of the content learned in earlier years is obsolete or no longer relevant. Now we must seek new content but we may not know *how*.

Think about your formal education. Think about how much content was stored in your memory and then retrieved at examination time. The information stored in your memory over the years undoubtedly would fill volumes. But is this what you really need? If you need certain bits of information at certain points in time, you undoubtedly can retrieve the information from a book or computer files. What you need most is a strategy for learning. You need process more than content.

The learning process can be mastered. There are many fine books that can contribute to this learning, but, in the final analysis, each person must develop and master his or her own learning process. Find your own preferred learning style, develop it, and put it to use.

Once you have mastered your own learning process, you may come to an important realization: many of your teachers, albeit innocently, gave you a fish when they should have been teaching you *how* to fish.

Knowing What is Important to Learn

With such a mass of documented knowledge, we must know what is important to learn. Take a day sometime to visit a large public library. The experience can be either uplifting or depressing, depending on your attitude. If you focus on the tremendous opportunity for learning, the experience can be uplifting. But if you focus on how very little of this accumulated knowledge you can acquire in your lifetime, the experience may be depressing.

Plato reportedly mastered most of the accumulated knowledge of his day. But that was almost 2500 years ago. What a different situation today. The amount of accumulated knowledge keeps expanding exponentially!

A question to ponder: What percent of the accumulated knowledge do you think that a given individual—a lifelong learner—can possibly acquire in a lifetime? I know of no conceivable way of making an accurate estimate. But I will hazard a guess: it will be no more than a small fraction of one percent.

This, then, becomes the central question: What will you include in your small fraction of one percent of the accumulated knowledge? What will be your learning strategy?

There are two routes for acquiring knowledge: the horizontal and the vertical. With the horizontal route, you remain on a lower plane accumulating more and more information, moving from one part of the library to the next. But you will find, eventually, as your friends begin to die off, that you are running out of time. By taking the vertical route, you rise through the layers of knowledge and take a systems view of knowledge. You move among the layers to acquire the desired knowledge—but guided by the systems view. Essentially, this is the difference between algorithmic learning and heuristic learning: the first includes detailed rules and procedures and the second encompasses general principles.

Developing Learning Goals

To stimulate your thinking about the learning process, here's a simple experiment. It is designed to answer this question: What percent of the adult population has clear learning goals? To answer the question, select ten adults at random: relatives, friends, or even strangers. Pose to each one this question: What are your learning goals for the next twelve-month period?

The results of this little experiment should prove interesting. A few of the individuals might appear puzzled by the question, and others might even laugh. My guess is that you will find very few people who have clear learning goals. They may indeed be learning new things, but they do not have clear learning goals.

Let's assume—confidently—that people who have clear learning goals will learn more than those lacking such goals. Yes, learning can occur in the absence of learning goals. All of us have had learning occur spontaneously in an unplanned situation. It happens and it is important. But there's more merit in having clear learning goals to guide this quest. Perhaps more important than increasing the *amount* of learning, learning goals enhance the *quality* of the learning. The outcome is that learning becomes more directed and more focused.

Set learning goals for yourself. These learning goals might relate to your job or career, to a hobby of interest to you, or to your own self-development. Then, with resolve, work toward the goals.

Seeking Opportunities for New Learning

With regard to learning, we each have a "comfort zone" in which we have mastered the knowledge required to function effectively. As a consequence, we feel comfortable and psychologically secure.

When the need for new learning requires that we go outside our own comfort zones, a certain amount of discomfort may arise. This demand for new learning may be perceived as a threat: we may look foolish, we may be embarrassed, and we may even fail. There is so much uncertainty.

There is a natural tension between the psychological security provided by remaining inside the comfort zone and the desire to explore outside the comfort zone. We witness this tension in our own development and growth. For example, if we are hiking and we advance to a ledge on the mountain, we remain there temporarily. We might need to muster up enough courage to advance to the next higher ledge. As we rest on a given ledge, we are in the static mode; as we move from one ledge to the next higher one, we are in the dynamic mode.

The lifelong learner achieves a good balance between the static and the dynamic. This person experiences new learning and takes the time to reflect on it and savor it, but then moves on to new learning opportunities. It's like moving from one ledge to the next, all the way up the mountain. In so doing, the comfort zone expands.

Reviewing What Was Learned

Life is made up of moving from one activity to the next. In the work place we complete one project and then move on to the next one. Or, more commonly, we don't actually complete the first project before we begin on the second. Then, at a later date, we return to complete the first project. This is the real world of schedules, deadlines, and changing priorities.

Because of the rush and pressure to move from one project to the next, we seldom take the time to reflect on what we learned from the experience on each project. Consequently, we miss out on a rich opportunity for learning.

After completing a given project, take the time to reflect on what was learned from the experience. Ask yourself: What new knowledge and skills have I acquired from this activity? What did I do well in this activity? What did I do not-so-well? If I were beginning the project today, what would I do differently? Honest and reflective answers to these questions promote action learning at its best.

Seeking Feedback

"Know thyself" was the inscription over the Oracle at Delphi centuries ago. Today, for anyone who aspires to be a lifelong learner, this inscription still serves as sound advice. To know ourselves is the most difficult task that any of us face. But the better we know ourselves, the better our potential for being effective learners.

Many of us resist receiving honest feedback from others. We carry in our consciousnesses an "ideal self"—the person that we would like to think that we are. Others see us as an "actual self"—the true self in their eyes. Not infrequently there are major discrepancies between the actual self as perceived by others and the ideal self as perceived (or desired) by ourselves. Honest feedback from others is then viewed as an attack, a threat to the ideal self. Consequently we reject the feedback.

In the quest for personal growth, this is the chain of causal relationships:

1. Personal growth depends on self-understanding.
2. Self-understanding depends on feedback from others.
3. Hence, personal growth depends on feedback from others.

This syllogism contains an important message: realize that the only way you will ever grow is to truly know your strengths and weaknesses. Further, the only way that you will truly know your strengths and weaknesses is to solicit honest feedback from others.

One way to get this feedback is to recruit four or five acquaintances who will be honest with you. Draw these acquaintances from among peers, people who report directly to you, your own manager, your spouse, and personal friends. There is one principal criterion for being a member of this feedback team: Every member must give *completely honest* feedback—positive or negative. Any member who continually praises and gives only positive feedback needs to be replaced. This could be the most important thing that you will ever do in advancing your own learning.

Learning From Your Mistakes

The learning model developed and promoted by B.F. Skinner, a behavioristic psychologist, focuses on successful performance in the learning process. Each learning situation is designed so that the learner can successfully master a chain of activities arranged in an ascending order of difficulty. Administering rewards appropriately for successful performance accelerates learning. This approach promotes success, success, and more success.

Certainly, there is nothing wrong with success—especially for building one's self-esteem. But as an essential factor in the learning process, we should not overlook the importance of our failures. Any number of highly effective leaders who have ascended to a higher rung on the learning ladder will tell you that their most beneficial learning came from their mistakes. And these people are sufficiently self-confident to admit their mistakes.

Individuals who are afraid of making mistakes will not take risks. They reside in their comfort zones clinging to one particular ledge and making no effort to climb to the next higher ledge. Consequently, they will not grow.

Assume that you will make mistakes—good, honest mistakes. But after each mistake, take the time to examine it and reflect upon it—and learn from it.

Willingness to Unlearn

In a paper titled, "Unlearning the Organization," Michael McGill and John Slocum offer these words of wisdom: "The first step to learning is to challenge those ways of thinking that worked so well in the past." They go on to say, "Unlearning makes way for new experiences and new ways of experiencing. It is the necessary precursor to learning." Indeed: we must unlearn in order to learn.

Consider the case of the amateur golfer who had taught herself how to play golf. She had been playing golf regularly for some five or six years before deciding to take lessons from a professional. At first, the instructor was very patient, trying to correct his student's awkward swing. As time went on, however, he began to lose his patience. After twelve lessons and absolutely no success in correcting the faulty swing, the instructor yelled in exasperation: "I wish that you had come to me when you first started playing golf!" And so it goes—both on and off the golf course.

We should be mindful of two different learning paradigms: the linear and the dynamic. The linear model says: we first learn A, then B, then C, and then D. Each builds on what went before, just as we would observe in the construction of a pyramid. The dynamic model carries a different message: we learned A at some point in the past, and now, to learn B, we must unlearn A.

An example of the need for unlearning is found when an organization attempts to transform itself from being a bureaucratic organization to being a learning organization. To effect this transition, managers in the organization must learn new behaviors associated with being a catalyst and *unlearn* those behaviors associated with being a controller.

Unlearning requires both skill and courage, but it can be done. It is an essential aspect of the learning process.

*

These guidelines that elucidate the art of knowing, or what we are calling the art of learning, are by no means all-inclusive or highly prescriptive. But they point the way.

Illuminating the Knowing mode in its totality, within the context of the Temple of Human Potential, what would we find if a given individual lives primarily in the Knowing apse and ignores the others? We would have an individual lacking real-world experience, core values, and an internal gyroscope for decision making. The result would be a "Walking Encyclopedia," an individual with lots of information and no way to use it. This would be a partially functioning human being. Only in conjunction with the other three modes can the Knowing mode be truly manifested.

THE ART OF BELIEVING

We move now from the Knowing mode to the Believing mode, from the objective to the subjective. These two modes of being, while quite different in makeup, are both essential to a fully functioning person.

Bertrand Russell, in *New Hopes for a Changing World*, provides a perspective:

> A way of life cannot be successful so long as it is a mere intellectual conviction. It must be deeply felt, deeply believed, dominant even in dreams.

Believing is being committed to and living by a set of core values. These values provide the spirit out of which we live, as well as the standards for judging our decisions and actions.

Values are like a musical score. If there were only a single musical score to guide us, our lives would be quite focused. But most people are handed various musical scores. Their religious institution offers them one score, their place of work a second, their family and friends still a third, and perhaps a fourth. The dilemma occurs because these musical scores may be competing and contradictory: it may be like listening to classical music, jazz, and country/western music simultaneously. Instead of music we have noise.

This "noise" results because many individuals have never thought deeply about their own personal values. They have never taken the time to really sort them out. As a consequence, they are pulled hither and yon by competing values.

In *The Nature of Human Values*, Milton Rokeach defines a *value* as "an enduring belief that a specific mode of conduct or end-state of existence is personally or socially preferable to an opposite or converse mode of conduct or end-state of existence." His *value system* is "an enduring organization of beliefs concerning preferable modes of conduct or end-states of existence along a continuum of relative importance."

Take note of several key points in these definitions. First, values are beliefs; they are not facts. Second, values are enduring; they are not evanescent. Third, values guide two aspects of our lives: our mode of conduct (or personal behavior) and our desired end-state of existence (or ultimate goals). And fourth, integrating a set of values into a real unity constitutes a value system.

Rokeach presents some clear examples and definitions of two different types of values, shown on the following two pages. *Terminal values* such as a sense of accomplishment, a world at peace, and social recognition may be viewed as *ends* toward which one is striving. *Instrumental values* such as ambition, broadmindedness, and competence may be viewed as *means* that one will employ to achieve the ends.

In a unified value system the ends and means are consistent and mutually reinforcing. For example, most would agree that a set of values that included the terminal values of "true friendship" and "mature love" and the instrumental values of "loving" and "forgiving" would be considered all of a piece.

Given the nature of human values, we can now focus more clearly on the Believing mode, where the fully functioning person is committed to and lives by a set of core values. The following approach illustrates how the fully functioning person might translate the Believing mode from theory into practice.

Socrates devoted much of his life to pondering and discussing this fundamental question: What is the essence of the good life? And, as mentioned previously, all of the major world religions have addressed the same question, teaching

Terminal Values

---

1. A COMFORTABLE LIFE	a prosperous life
2. AN EXCITING LIFE	a stimulating, active life
3. A SENSE OF ACCOMPLISHMENT	lasting contribution
4. A WORLD AT PEACE	free of war and conflict
5. A WORLD OF BEAUTY	beauty of nature and the arts
6. EQUALITY	brotherhood, equal opportunity for all
7. FAMILY SECURITY	taking care of loved ones
8. FREEDOM	independence, free choice
9. HAPPINESS	contentedness
10. INNER HARMONY	freedom from inner conflict
11. MATURE LOVE	sexual and spiritual intimacy
12. NATIONAL SECURITY	protection from attack
13. PLEASURE	an enjoyable, leisurely life
14. SALVATION	saved, eternal life
15. SELF-RESPECT	self-esteem
16. SOCIAL RECOGNITION	respect, admiration
17. TRUE FRIENDSHIP	close companionship
18. WISDOM	a mature understanding of life

Milton Rokeach—*The Nature of Human Values*

Instrumental Values

1.	AMBITIOUS	hard-working, aspiring
2.	BROADMINDED	open-minded
3.	CAPABLE	competent, effective
4.	CHEERFUL	lighthearted, joyful
5.	CLEAN	neat, tidy
6.	COURAGEOUS	standing up for your beliefs
7.	FORGIVING	willing to pardon others
8.	HELPFUL	working for the welfare of others
9.	HONEST	sincere, truthful
10.	IMAGINATIVE	daring, creative
11.	INDEPENDENT	self-reliant, self-sufficient
12.	INTELLECTUAL	intelligent, reflective
13.	LOGICAL	consistent, rational
14.	LOVING	affectionate, tender
15.	OBEDIENT	dutiful, respectful
16.	POLITE	courteous, well-mannered
17.	RESPONSIBLE	dependable, reliable
18.	SELF-CONTROLLED	restrained, self-disciplined

Milton Rokeach—*The Nature of Human Values*

and promoting the values associated with their particular views of the good life.

The question of the good life is the kernel within the husk. We must remove the husk if we are to get at our core values.

Assume that you are Almustafa, the central personage in Kahlil Gibran's *The Prophet*. You have been the beloved guest of the people of Orphalese. After spending twelve years with these gentle and kindly people, you are now preparing to leave and return to the isle of your birth. Before you leave, the people of Orphalese want you to share more of your wisdom with them. This is their final question: What is the good life?

What would be your response to the people of Orphalese? What is your view of the good life?

Based on your view of the good life, can you identify the underlying values? What particular values define the good life—as you see it. Have you identified both terminal values and instrumental values? Are the values all of a piece?

This initial list of values may contain both core values and peripheral values. Which ones are most important to you personally? Which ones are central?

Reflect on how your own core values might have come into existence. Identify what you consider to be the contributing influences, for example, your religious institution, your parents, your teachers, your friends and associates, your favorite authors. Were there special persons who had a significant influence on your life? Which influences contributed to which values? Can you find the central threads?

We each carry within us two sets of values: espoused values and operational values. Espoused values are those that we *say* are important to us. Operational values are those that we *put into practice*, those that we actually live by. This next step requires some real soul-searching. What are the discrepancies between your espoused values and your operational values? And to overcome your own blind spots, seek feedback from others.

If you have worked through the exercise up to this point, then you should be prepared to take this next important step. Select those core values that you can truly commit yourself to. These are the espoused-values-made-operational, which means that the espoused values and the operational values are one and the same. What you believe intellectually will be made manifest in your actions and deeds.

If your values are arranged simply as a list, they may have only minimal influence on your life. In times of stress—when you most need the guidance of your values—it may be difficult to sort out what is on the list. Thus, it is essential that you have a central thread, a theme, that runs through the entire set of values. In the words of Sören Kierkegaard: "Purity of heart is to will one thing." It is this "one thing" that helps you center your life. What is the central theme of your life?

In *The Nichomachean Ethics*, Aristotle stresses the importance of practice:

> But the virtues we acquire by first exercising them, as is the case with all the arts, for it is by doing what we ought to do when we have learnt the arts that we learn the arts themselves; we become, e.g., builders by building and harpists by playing the harp. Similarly it is by doing just acts that we become just, by doing temperate acts that we become temperate, by doing courageous acts that we become courageous.

And so it is with your own personal values. For those values to be real values—to be an integral and enduring part of your character—you must live the values daily.

Benjamin Franklin, the great American statesman, made a habit of reviewing, at the end of each day, how well he had achieved the goals that he had set for himself for that particular day. In like manner, at the end of each day think about how well you lived your values that particular day. If you went astray, ask yourself why. And ask yourself what you might do to correct or at least improve the situation in the future. If you did well, congratulate yourself. Anyone who conscientiously carries out this process over an extended period of time will undoubtedly improve the link between espoused values and operational values.

Rokeach defines a value as an "enduring belief." This is true if we consider enduring to mean continuing and lasting, not transient. But it does not necessarily mean that one's values should be "set in concrete" for evermore. As we learn and grow, we change. As we move out of our comfort zones, we change. As we advance from one ledge on the mountain to the next higher ledge, we change. Thus, we should periodically reexamine our core values. Are the values that we held to some ten years ago still the same values that we hold to today? It's a point to ponder.

*

This discussion expands on the Believing mode, but is by no means all-inclusive or prescriptive in terms of what your values should be. The focus has been on process, not content.

Consider the Believing mode in its totality, within the context of the Temple of Human Potential. If a given individual lives primarily in the Believing mode and looks askance at the other three modes, we would have a person lacking real-world experience, objective knowledge, and an internal gyroscope for decision making. The result would be what Eric Hoffer calls the "True Believer," an individual who has confused beliefs and facts and, consequently, is convinced that there is only one path to the top of the mountain. At best, this would be a partially functioning human being. Only in conjunction with the other three modes can the Believing mode be fully realized.

THE ART OF BEING

Being is defined here as achieving selfhood, authentic personal existence. Gautama Buddha shows the way: "Be lamps unto yourselves. Work out your own salvation with diligence."

Echoing Buddha in the book, *To Have Or To Be?*, Erich Fromm provides a perspective:

> The anxiety and insecurity engendered by the danger of losing what one has are absent in the being mode. If *I am who I am* and not what I have, nobody can deprive me or threaten my security and my sense of identity. My center is within myself; my capacity for being and for expressing my essential powers is part of my character structure and depends on me.

We are inclined to revere those who live in the Being mode. Consider the world's great teachers: Buddha, Confucius, Jesus, the Prophet Muhammad, and Socrates. They were independent and authentic persons of the first order. They indeed lived out of the Being mode. For ordinary people, however, there is considerable psychological risk associated with this mode of existence. Each of the other three modes provides us something tangible: Coping mode—concrete reality; Knowing mode—objective knowledge; Believing mode—the values of the community. But in the Being mode we have only our own self-beings to hold onto. This is more freedom than some individuals desire or can even endure. And there will be some who prefer to return to the security of the cave depicted in Plato's famous parable.

The fully functioning person lives out of the Being mode as a truly independent and authentic person. What guides this person's life?

The Courage To Be

In *The Courage to Be*, Paul Tillich defines courage:

Courage is the affirmation of one's essential nature, but it is an affirmation which has in itself the character of "in spite of." It includes the possible and, in some cases, the unavoidable sacrifice of elements which also belong to one's being but which, if not sacrificed, would prevent us from reaching our actual fulfillment.

To truly understand what Tillich is saying, let's consider his basic ideas one by one.

Courage is the affirmation of one's authentic self. You have an inner self that only you really know; this is your authentic self. You also have an outer self that is projected to others; this is your persona. The person of courage asserts his or her authentic self.

Courage is the affirmation that is made "in spite of." In affirming your authentic self, you will sometimes encounter obstacles and resistance. There may be some individuals who do not want you to be your authentic self, because they may be threatened by your authenticity. Nevertheless, the person of courage will assert his or her authentic self.

Courage involves sacrificing peripheral desires. Picture in your mind's eye a large center circle and then several smaller circles on its periphery. The large circle represents your authentic self, and the smaller circles represent peripheral desires. For various individuals, peripheral desires might include being wealthy, having prestige, being accepted by others, being successful, winning at sports, and so forth. For the individual who lacks courage, the center of gravity for one's life can shift from the center circle to one of the peripheral circles. But not so with the person of courage. This person will sacrifice peripheral circles in order to maintain the center of gravity within the center circle.

In the act of courage, the most important part of one's being prevails over the others. The fully functioning person firmly grasps his or her priorities in life. This person knows what is very important, what is moderately important, and what is unimportant . . . and sets a course accordingly.

Courage is the readiness to take upon oneself negatives for the sake of a fuller positivity. Most people are disturbed when they are rejected by others—especially friends. And most people do not like to have their ideas criticized by persons of knowledge. But the person of courage will bear such negatives for the greater good—namely, to remain an authentic person.

The Oracle at Delphi advised each person to "know thyself." But equally important, we should heed the words of Paul Tillich: "Be thyself in spite of obstacles." *Have the courage to be.*

The Internal Gyroscope

The sociological studies of David Riesman have acquainted many of us with the concepts of inner-directed and other-directed social character. In *The Lonely Crowd*, Riesman describes other-directed persons as ones who use their contemporaries as their source of direction—either those known personally or those known indirectly through friends or the mass media. Other-directed persons pay close attention to the signals from others. In contrast, inner-directed persons are ones who are guided by internal gyroscopes that keep them "on course" and help them withstand the buffeting of the external environment.

Be an inner-directed person. Let your internal gyroscope be your locus of control.

Being Your Own Philosopher

Philosophy is not the exclusive property of professional philosophers; it is open to all. Philosophy is not simply an academic subject; it is a way of life. The philosopher is one who asks the most fundamental questions about life and then puts considerable effort into answering the questions. The philosopher is guided by reason in a search for truth.

You can be your own philosopher. Spend time in each of the six chambers of the Temple of Humanity: the atrium, the four apses, and even the cellar. Reflect on these four questions: (1) What does it mean to be human? (2) What can we know? (3) What should we do? and (4) What may we hope for? Then come up with your own answers. Develop your own philosophy of life—and then live the philosophy of life.

Importance of the Questions

Jeane Kirkpatrick, former U.S. ambassador to the United Nations, makes special note of asking the right questions:

> Not long after (my life became ordered), it occurred to me that perhaps I had been spending time on the wrong questions. Instead of asking "What is the meaning of life?" perhaps I should have been asking "What will give my life meaning?"*

In being your own philosopher, asking questions is one of the most important aspects of the journey. Be curious. Ask questions. Ask good questions. Ask lots of questions. Consider the questions to be as important as the answers.

---

*In *Living Philosophies,* edited by Clifton Fadiman.

Systems Thinking

Why is systems thinking such a rarity? In the popular book *The Fifth Discipline*, Peter Senge elucidates the problem: "From a very early age, we are taught to break apart problems, to fragment the world. This apparently makes complex tasks and subjects more manageable, but we pay a hidden enormous price. We can no longer see the consequences of our actions; we lose our intrinsic sense of connection to a larger whole." Senge pinpoints a major problem: Many of us have been taught to analyze and understand the individual trees in the forest, but in the process we have lost sight of the forest.

To help leaders move from such highly specialized thinking to systems thinking, Senge offers several guiding principles:

1. The essence of mastering systems thinking lies in seeing patterns where others see only events and forces to react to.

2. Systems thinking means translating a complex situation into a coherent story that illuminates the causes of problems and how they can be remedied in enduring ways.

3. Systems thinking finds its greatest benefits in helping us distinguish high-leverage from low-leverage changes in highly complex situations.

4. Nothing happens until there is vision—which stimulates movement from the status quo.

5. Vision without systems thinking ends up painting lovely pictures of the future with no deep understanding of the forces that must be mastered to move from here to there.

Be a systems thinker. Remove the separator walls from your memory bank. Climb to the top of the pyramid and gaze down at the total edifice.

Analyzing the Assumptions

Assumptions are things that we simply take for granted. They often take on a life of their own.

Understand and appreciate that all of our views are based on certain assumptions, presuppositions. The assumptions may be either explicit or implicit, but they are indeed ever-present.

Take the time to analyze the assumptions underlying your views. Why do you view a particular situation or phenomenon as you do? When discussing a specific issue with another person, share your underlying assumptions. And ask that person to challenge your assumptions.

Practically every viewpoint is based on assumptions. To truly understand different viewpoints—either your own or those of others—you must examine the underlying assumptions.

Seeking Criticism of Your Ideas

Be willing to subject your reasoning to criticism. When looking for reactions to your ideas, don't just seek out friends and supporters. We know in advance that our comrades will endorse our ideas and give us the desired praise. And we probably know implicitly that an automatic endorsement of our ideas will contribute little to their development.

Individuals who are committed to a life of reason will actively seek out those who will question and challenge their ideas. In pursuing truth, these individuals desire every possible insight.

Open-Mindedness

Open-mindedness is the willingness to try to understand different points of view. It does not necessarily mean that we agree with them.

Our open-mindedness grows when we make a sincere effort to become aware of other views. We can be sensitive to the fact that there are diverse views on every major issue—religion, politics, leadership, success, and on and on. Our awareness of these diverse views grows by being attentive: by reading, by observing, by questioning. We can seek out individuals who hold views different from our own. We should be hesitant to evaluate any particular view as being either right or wrong, but simply be attentive to the diversity and richness of these views.

Our open-mindedness also will be enhanced if we make a sincere effort to truly understand these diverse views. What is this person trying to say? Why does this person view the situation this way? In all truthfulness, is my own view on this issue any more valid than this other person's views?

We can still take a firm stand, but only after considering opposing ideas.

Seeking Mutual Understanding

In the domain of interpersonal communication, we observe two radically different approaches: debate and dialogue. Note the difference in the roots of these two words: The root of debate is to "beat down"; the root of dialogue is the "flow of meaning." Also note the difference in goals: the goal of debate is to achieve victory; the goal of dialogue is to achieve mutual understanding.

The art of philosophizing is grounded in dialogue. When we find two authentic persons engaged in honest and open communication, there are no hidden agendas and no trickery; everything is out on the table and aboveboard. There is mutual respect for the other's views and a mutual search for truth. This is communication at its best.

Enjoying the Journey

Life is not an end-state, but a journey. In the paper "Explorations in Essential Being," Clark Moustakas states it well when he says:

The person who expresses his unique nature enjoys the getting to some place, as well as the arriving. Even when there is a goal, the entire process of pursuing or moving in its direction is important, and as much a value as the *goal* itself.

Living in the Being mode is a lifelong journey. Enjoy the journey!

*

In summarizing the Being mode, the guidelines presented are by no means all-inclusive nor are they highly prescriptive. But they may point the way.

It is instructive to illuminate the Being mode in its totality, within the context of the Temple of Human Potential. What would we find if a given individual lives primarily in the Being mode and is indifferent to the other three modes? We would have an individual who lacks real-world experience, objective knowledge, and core values. We would have a "Rebel Without a Cause," an individual totally committed to independence and authenticity but lacking in substance and direction. This would be a partially functioning human being. Only in conjunction with the other three modes can the Being mode be fully realized.

* * * * *

Now we have our leader described as a fully functioning person. Building on the framework provided by the Temple of Humanity, we have constructed the Temple of Human Potential. This temple, with its atrium and four apses, is an outline of human potential, symbolizing what each person can become. The framework provided by the temple is a response to the question: What does it mean to be human?

The fully functioning person resides in the total temple. By being centered in the Art of Living and by incorporating the realms of Coping, Knowing, Believing, and Being, any

79

individual can become a fully functioning person. Such persons are rare, *but they do exist*. And, potentially, they might be found in any and every village or hamlet of the world.

The challenge for leaders in the world community is to become fully functioning persons and to help others become fully functioning persons. The two are synergistic. By becoming a fully functioning person, you will likely enhance the personal development of others. And by enhancing the personal development of others, you will enhance your own development.

IV

WAY TO WISDOM

Say not, "I have found *the* truth," but rather,
"I have found *a* truth."

KAHLIL GIBRAN
The Prophet

I n the second of the fundamental questions: What can we know?, the focus is on the meaning of—and the quest for—truth.

The word "truth" has a special appeal to it. We search for it and we rejoice when we think we have found it. Truth seems to be what is of utmost importance.

To the great Indian leader, Mahatma Gandhi, God was Truth and Truth was God. Truth and God were one and the same. What could be a more noble quest than the quest for truth?

Truth supports each of us . . . all of us. Without truth to guide us, we are like a ship without a steering mechanism.

The quest for a global ethic must be grounded in a reasonable view of truth. And this view of truth must be reasonable not only to you and me, but to peoples around the world. Achieving such a goal would be much more than a mere milestone along the way; it would be a giant step toward furthering dialogue and mutual understanding among peoples of diverse origins and backgrounds.

The question of truth was one of Kant's four fundamental questions: What can I know? We restate it: What can we know?

Kant's inquiry focused on understanding the relation between the subjective thinker and the thought object. You and I, as subjective thinkers, see the world and try to make sense out of it. But our thinking cannot be done in a vacuum; there must be an object of thought, such as a physical object, an experience, an event, or even a concept. Even though the thinking subject and the thought object are closely coupled, we feel certain that they are different entities. What is the relation between the two? That was Kant's pressing question.

To tackle the question, let's review the definitions of three terms:

- Reality: the quality or state of being real, actual.
- Truth: conformity to what is real or actual.
- Knowledge: apprehending truth.

Now back to Kant's question: What is the relation between the subjective thinker and the thought object? The thought object is reality. Truth is that which conforms to the thought object. And a grasp of this truth is knowledge.

What can we know? We can know truth. And what is truth? Conformity to what is real or actual. Thus, our route to what is real or actual is through truth. There is no other way.

Given these basics, we now return to the question, What can we know? To address the question, we need a framework or context.

Perhaps we cannot answer the question, What can we *know?* through *knowledge.* We are reminded of the old adage: "The eye cannot see the eye." But with wisdom perhaps we can find answers.

THE TEMPLE OF WISDOM

In my own quest to look beyond knowledge to wisdom, I have asked a number of people to define wisdom. These are some of the responses:

- "It is more than mere intellect."
- "It is more than knowledge."

- "It is common sense with depth."
- "It is good judgment."
- "It is the ability to put things in perspective."
- "It is intellect plus experience."
- "It is the rational plus the intuitive."

Webster's Dictionary offers this definition of wisdom: ability to discern inner qualities of relationships; great understanding of people and of situations and unusual discernment and judgment in dealing with them.

The Random House Dictionary has a somewhat different definition: knowledge of what is true or right coupled with just judgment as to action. The notion of "true or right" suggests that wisdom contains both a rational dimension and a moral dimension.

Given these preliminary ideas about the nature of wisdom, we can construct a framework. The Temple of Humanity translates into the Temple of Wisdom on the following page. This is the alignment between corresponding chambers in the two temples:

- Humanitas: Mental Models
- Daily Life: Experience
- Science: Observation
- Religion: Faith
- Philosophy: Reason

With mental models serving as the centerpiece, the temple provides four distinct paths to truth: experience, observation, faith, and reason. Truth can be found in each of these chambers.

Where can we find wisdom? Wisdom is defined by the total temple. Wisdom is grasping the *whole* of truth.

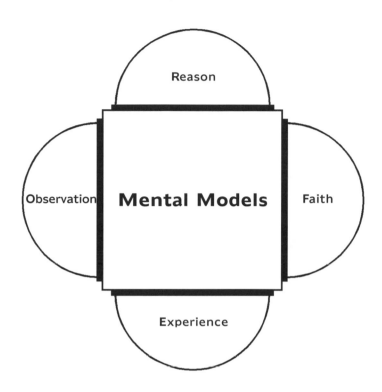

The Temple of Wisdom

Given this fundamental premise, let's examine each of the five chambers, keeping in mind the temple as a whole; otherwise we will be contemplating something other than wisdom.

MENTAL MODELS

The atrium of the Temple of Wisdom represents mental models, which are constellations of assumptions and generalizations about some aspect of the world.

In *A Theory of Personality*, George Kelly provides a more succinct description of mental models:

> Man looks at his world through transparent patterns or templets which he creates and then attempts to fit over the realities of which the world is composed. The fit is not always very good. Yet without such patterns the world appears to be such an undifferentiated homogeneity that man is unable to make any sense of it. Even a poor fit is more helpful to him than nothing at all.

The transparent pattern or templet is the mental model. It represents reality—as created by the individual and carried mentally—to make sense out of some aspect of the world. And it is apparent that some fits will be better than others. But regardless of the goodness of fit, it also is apparent that the individual would be unable to function in the world without such mental models.

With a definition of mental models, we can now grasp the locus of truth. So if reality is the quality or state of being real or actual, truth is the conformity to what is real or actual. Thus, if the mental model conforms to reality, it is true. If it does not conform to reality, it is untrue. Or even better: a mental model is true to the degree that it conforms to reality. The key point: the essence of truth is found in the relationship between the mental model and reality.

Mental models follow the rules of general semantics. General semanticists use "maps" and "territory" to refer, respectively, to words and the objects denoted by the words. For example: the word "cow" and an actual cow are two different things; the word "leader" and an actual leader are two different things; the U.S. President saying, "The economy is thriving" and a thriving economy are two different things. Maps and territory are two different entities, and we should not confuse them. Similarly, with mental models and reality:

these are two different entities, and we should not mistake one for the other.

Now, returning to Kant's pressing question: What is the relationship between the thinking subject and the thought object? We have an answer: It is the relationship between a mental model and reality. The mental model connects the subjective thinker and the object of thought.

Our quest for truth should encourage us to understand the nature of mental models. We should understand that our mental models are transparent patterns or templets that connect us to reality. And how close we are to reality is a function of how closely our mental models align to reality.

Understanding the concept of mental models is an initial step in approaching truth and reality. But we must go beyond this initial step to examine and explore mental models. We should scrutinize our own mental models, examining very carefully the underlying assumptions and generalizations. And we should inquire into others' mental models, which will help us appreciate the diversity in mental models as well as enhance our own mental models.

Then we can better understand the four basic paths to truth: experience, observation, faith, and reason. So we will now leave the atrium and journey to the four apses.

EXPERIENCE

Personal experience is an important path to truth. It is one apse in the Temple of Wisdom.

The importance of experience as a path to truth is explained by the psychologist Abraham Maslow in his book *The Psychology of Science*:

> My toothache feels different from your toothache. And so it goes. Perhaps it is better to say that all of life must first be

known experientially. There is no substitute for experience, none at all.

Now just suppose that Maslow's dentist had disagreed with him. After carefully examining the X-ray, the dentist is convinced that there is no problem. But Maslow insists that he does indeed have a very painful toothache. Who would you believe: the dentist or the patient? Who is closer to the truth?

Living experience is our closest contact with reality. Our jobs, our family lives, and our hobbies draw us close to reality. And our joys and our sorrows also draw us close to reality. These are the really real.

We hear the old-timer say, "Experience is the best teacher." There is much wisdom in this admonition. Old-timers know, because they have benefited greatly from their many years of practical experience.

Consider the young woman who wants to learn how to swim. She reads books on swimming; she fills her day by observing swimmers; and she fills her evenings by discussing swimming. But this young woman will never learn how to swim until she jumps into the water and tries it.

Consider the young man who desires to be an effective leader. Seminars on leadership will help; reading books on leadership will help; and observing effective leaders will help. But he will not learn how to be an effective leader until he practices being a leader.

Then, finally, consider the young couple who desire to be effective parents. They can attend lectures on parenting; they can read books on parenting; and they can join a discussion group on effective parenting. But they will not learn how to be effective parents until they practice parenting with their own children.

And so it goes. A variety of activities can contribute to the learning, but real learning occurs in real-world experience. The old-timer was right: "Experience is the best teacher."

In reflecting on the importance of experience, consider the possibility of going into battle. If you are a soldier of your country, you will be expected to go into the jungle to engage in hand-to-hand combat with enemy troops. You can now choose which of two leaders you will follow into the jungle. One is a first lieutenant who has just graduated from the military academy. Being first in his class, he graduated with high honors. And he received accolades for his graduate thesis that analyzed Clausewitz's great work on the nature of war and strategy. The other is a master sergeant who has completed twenty years of military service. Five years of this service have been spent in the jungle fighting the enemy. Which of the two leaders would you choose to follow? I personally would go with the master sergeant.

Most of us admire those individuals who are known for their common sense. They have had a great deal of practical experience and, through good judgment, can apply the experience to everyday affairs.

Each of us, to function effectively in the world, needs both applied knowledge and theoretical knowledge. Theories provide perspective, general concepts, and a framework for understanding. But theoretical knowledge by itself is inadequate. Until it is tested in the crucible of everyday life, it will be found lacking.

Practical experience serves as a touchstone for the theoretical. Until the theoretical is tested in everyday life, it will remain tentative.

In the domain of experience, where is truth? The pragmatist says truth is found in satisfying and practical consequences. We look at the results of our efforts and judge the consequences. Were they favorable? If so, then we can conclude that our efforts were right and true.

Most of us will agree that some of the deepest truths are found in our own personal experiences. Granted it is a sample of only one, but we often feel that what is happening to us personally is the closest thing to ultimate reality and truth. Some experiences are deep and filled with meaning. To us, this is truth.

But we need more than the raw experience to truly benefit from it. To expand our understanding of applied knowledge, we need a variety of experiences, and we need to reflect on the experiences. Reflecting and examining can transform a thin mental model into a rich mental model.

Consider the case of Albert. He spent his entire life in a single valley where he was born. With only a few years of formal schooling, Albert had little interest in reading or in finding out what was beyond the perimeter of the valley. So he never ventured outside the valley. He did indeed understand what was going on inside the valley and he had enough basic knowledge and skills to earn a decent living. But his mental models were extremely limited in breadth and depth. Moreover, with regard to the "is" and the "ought," there was no difference. To Albert, *what was* was synonymous with *what should be*. Now contrast Albert with Immanuel Kant, one of the greatest philosophers of all time. This brilliant philosopher only once in his life traveled beyond the boundary of East Prussia. His worldly knowledge came from constant reading, reflection, and imagination. Karl Jaspers, in his biography of Kant, reported that, in conversation with a visiting Englishman, Kant spoke so vividly of St. Peter's that the other was convinced he had been to Rome.

Albert and Kant make an interesting contrast. The one thing they have in common is their limited travel beyond their place of birth. But the similarity ends there. Albert had years of practical experience, but, because of the absence of reflection and imagination, had only restricted mental models of the world. Now Kant had no more practical experience than Albert, but, because of his deep reflection and rich imagination, was able to transcend his environs and create rich and expansive mental models of the world.

Experience, by itself, is not sufficient to serve as a principal way of knowing. Something more is needed—breadth of experience, reflection on the experience, and imagination. Experience is a definite stage in our understanding of things, but we need to go further.

OBSERVATION

Observation as used by the empirical scientist is an important path to truth. It is one apse of the Temple.

We ask: What is science? The layperson might answer by naming specific fields of science, such as physics, chemistry, biology, and so on. Or a more sophisticated response might be to list the broad areas of science, such as the physical sciences, the natural sciences, the life sciences, the social sciences, and so forth.

The professional scientist will challenge the response. Science is not defined by its subject matter, but by its method. The scientific method is the common feature of all specific fields of science, and it is the essence of science.

Some fields of study lend themselves to the scientific method better than others. Physics, chemistry, and geology, for example, are most amenable to the scientific method. Psychology, sociology, and cultural anthropology, on the other hand, are more tenuous. But all six fields are sciences— because the scientific method aids in the quest for truth and knowledge.

Then there are some fields of endeavor, such as psychotherapy, that are on the borderline. The psychotherapist typically would use empirical findings in dealing with mental illness, but the particular application of this knowledge in treating a given patient requires a great deal of art. Thus, psychotherapy might be considered more of an art than a science.

The essence of science is found in its method. Ralph Thomas, a colleague of mine, captured the fundamental nature of empirical science in this easy-to-remember name of a hypothetical man: "MR. P.V." Each letter in the name represents an important feature of the scientific method, and the four letters combined capture the essence of the scientific method. The "M" stands for *measure*, which is to quantify selected variables. The "R" stands for *relate*, which is to determine the nature of the relationships between and among the quantified variables. The "P" stands for *predict*, which is to declare in advance the expected outcome. And the "V" stands for *verify*, which is to establish the accuracy of the prediction. MR.P.V.: measure, relate, predict, and verify— the fundamental nature of the scientific method.

To highlight the objectivity of the scientific method, Max Weber, the German sociologist, stressed the importance of separating empirical findings and values. His proposal is valid up to a point. Obviously, the scientific community is guided by certain core values, such as objectivity, predictability, and verifiability. Without such values to serve as guiding principles, science would not be science. But Weber correctly asserted that the scientist must not allow his or her personal values to influence the interpretation of empirical findings. Even findings contrary to the scientist's personal values and desires must be reported honestly and accurately.

By reporting the facts honestly and accurately, the results of one study will build on the results of previous studies. Scientific knowledge thus grows like a pyramid, from the base up. Each new bit of knowledge adds another stone to the pyramid. And this is why the credibility of scientific reporting is of utmost importance. One chink in the pyramid would threaten its robustness—and validity.

Where is truth? To the scientist, truth is found in compelling certainty of the facts. If the scientist has adhered faithfully to the process of measuring, relating, predicting, and verifying, then the facts do indeed provide compelling certainty.

Facts are essential to the scientific enterprise, but the scientist must go beyond the raw facts. Facts uninterpreted would be a hodgepodge of meaningless data. To make sense out of the facts, the scientist builds theories that begin with facts and end with facts. The theory helps interpret and explain the facts.

Credible scientists hold their theories tentatively. In the book, *A Philosopher Looks at Science*, John Kemeny puts it this way:

> A scientist holds his theories tentatively, always prepared to abandon them if the facts do not bear out the predictions. If a series of observations, designed to verify certain predictions, force us to abandon our theory, then we look for a new or improved theory.

In developing scientific theories, there is a gradual transition from mental models to paradigms. The individual scientist creates a theory—or mental model—of some aspect of the world. Once accepted and widely shared by a community of scientists, it is then considered a paradigm. Darwin's theory of evolution and Einstein's theory of relativity are excellent cases in point.

We must remind ourselves that the paradigm—or mental model—is not reality *per se*. It *represents reality*. The better the fit, the closer to reality. And the truth of the paradigm is universally valid: it is true for all of humanity, from Scotland to South Africa to Bangladesh.

Even though we might be upset or distressed by certain scientific theories, we must be willing to accept them as one avenue to truth. Perhaps certain scientific findings challenge cherished beliefs, as did both the Copernican theory of the universe and the Darwinian theory of evolution in their day. But avoiding scientific truth leads to untruthfulness. We now know, for example, that the Pope wrongly charged Galileo with heresy for espousing the Copernican theory of the universe. But did you know that, some 350 years later, the Vatican did offer a formal retraction and apology?

Today it is important—and urgent—that the general public understand the nature of scientific truth and be able to interpret scientific findings. Ordinary people need to be sufficiently versed in science to make sense out of the numerous scientific studies reported in the popular press. These findings influence our lives in numerous ways, and we must be able to make intelligent decisions regarding their application.

In understanding the role of science in our lives, we are reminded of the difference between the empirical and the normative. The empirical refers to the "is" and the normative to the "ought." Science is limited to the "is" side of the equation. Something beyond science must provide the "ought." But once this is done, then science can often tell us how to get there. Even though there are core values intrinsic to science, science cannot provide humanity with ultimate goals or values.

Thus, we can conclude that scientific truth is one important way of knowing, but it is not the only way. It is an important apse in the Temple of Wisdom, but it is not the total temple.

FAITH

Faith is an important path to truth. It is one apse of the Temple of Wisdom.

As we travel from the west apse of the temple to the east apse, we are moving from the empirical to the normative, from the "is" to the "ought." Empirical science is limited to the "is"; it cannot provide us with the "ought." Some other mode of knowing is required, and this mode of knowing is commonly called faith.

The Danish theologian/philosopher Sören Kierkegaard often made reference to "the leap of faith." Kierkegaard believed that his empirical knowledge and his reason would take him only so far in his quest for truth and fulfillment. These two ways of knowing were necessary—but not sufficient. Only by taking a "leap" beyond empirical knowledge and reason could he arrive at the desired destination. And this leap was based upon faith.

Paul Tillich viewed faith as ultimate concern. Faith is what is of utmost importance to us; it is the ultimate why in our lives. Everything else is subordinate to this ultimate why. Tillich cautioned us to not allow subordinate concerns to become our ultimate concern, which can readily happen if we allow material possessions and sensory pleasures to dominate our lives. We must make certain that the principal concern in our everyday lives is truly ultimate. Building on Tillich's idea of faith as ultimate concern, we can define faith as *a commitment to valued ends*. The valued ends are our ultimate concern, and our commitment is our active devotion to these ends. We look out at the world in our quest for meaning, and we find meaning in selected valued ends. The link between us and the valued ends is our personal commitment and active devotion. This commitment constitutes our faith.

In *The Quest for Identity*, Allen Wheelis states it well when he says:

> To commit allegiance and will and energy to valued ends means to define the self in terms of these ends and to find in them the enduring meaning and purpose in life.

In one cogent sentence, Wheelis has captured both the meaning and value of faith. The meaning of faith: to commit allegiance and will and energy to valued ends. The value of faith: it helps define the self in terms of these ends and to find in them the enduring meaning and purpose in life.

What are these valued ends? Where do we find them? For many persons, the valued ends are found in a particular paradigm—a constellation of beliefs, values, and guiding principles—generally accepted by a given community.

Historically, we find many examples of well known personages committed to a particular paradigm. Those early Greek philosophers, Socrates, Plato, and Aristotle, were committed to philosophy as a way of life. The great church fathers, St. Augustine and St. Thomas, were committed to the Christian religion. Those preeminent scientists, Copernicus, Galileo, and Newton, were committed to science. Their commitments were totally devoted to a given paradigm. This commitment was their faith.

In the modern era, we can grasp the essence of faith by reflecting on how we as individuals relate to our respective religions. If we adopt a particular religious paradigm—Buddhism, Christianity, Hinduism, Islam, Judaism, or some other—and we are genuinely committed to this paradigm through our allegiance, will, and energy—then this is our faith. Our faith is the connecting link between us and the paradigm.

The paradigm is represented by our individualized mental models. Given that the paradigm is owned by the community at large and the mental model is owned by the individual, each person's bond with the paradigm is via the mental model. Each person carries his or her own particular interpretation of the paradigm in the mental model. Because no two individuals carry exactly the same mental model in their heads, we are inclined to agree with Gandhi when he says, "There are as many different religions as there are people."

There also are two radically different approaches to adopting a particular religious paradigm. Erich Fromm, in *Man for Himself*, clearly differentiates rational faith and irrational faith. Rational faith is that which has been examined, reflected upon, and chosen in one's own freedom. Irrational faith is that which has been passed down and accepted blindly. Given this distinction, we can say that people are either once-born or twice-born with respect to their religious faith. Once-born individuals simply "go with the flow" and follow the religion of their forebears without examining or questioning. Those who are twice-born leave the flow, so to speak, examine the particular faith, reflect on it, and freely choose to adopt it. The latter are of strong faith; the former are not.

In describing faith in terms of paradigms and mental models, the question then becomes: Where is truth? To answer the question, we must clarify the difference between objective truth and subjective truth. Objective truth is based upon observable facts and is universally valid—for all of humanity. Subjective truth is personal truth; it is valid for the individual person. For example: My understanding of the theory of relativity is objective truth, whereas my commitment to a particular religion is subjective truth—it is true for me. Separating truth into these two categories by no means suggests that one is superior to the other. It simply affirms that there are these two distinctly different types of truth and, further, that the way to wisdom requires a deep understanding of both.

The reality of subjective truth is captured very well in Hans Küng's concept of relative absoluteness, which was mentioned in Chapter II. My particular faith is relative to me specifically in terms of my particular mental model, and is relative to my community insofar as we members are committed to the same paradigm. Even though my faith does not represent universal truth, it nevertheless is absolutely true for me; it is indubitably true for me. It is my ultimate concern.

Then where is truth? With respect to faith, truth is found in the conviction that a particular paradigm is true for me.

This view of truth in faith should encourage us to respect the truth of others. I have my faith, and you have yours. My faith is true for me, and your faith is true for you. I will certainly acknowledge your right to hold fast to your faith and I trust that you will do likewise with me.

So faith is an important apse in the Temple of Wisdom. Whereas empirical knowledge provides us with the "is," faith provides us with the "ought." They are complementary—not contradictory—apses of the temple. Both are essential in our quest for wisdom.

REASON

Reason is an important path to truth. It is one apse of the Temple of Wisdom.

As we begin to examine the nature of reason, we can "reflect" on the words of Socrates:

> Knowledge does not reside in the impressions, but in our reflection upon them. It is there, seemingly, and not in the impressions, that it is possible to grasp existence and truth.*

We can have impression after impression from sensory perceptions, but the knowledge embedded in these impressions remains latent until the impressions have been reflected upon, or processed. The reflection is what lifts the impression from lower consciousness (or even unconsciousness) to higher consciousness. This is the essence of reason, which is qualitatively different from experience per se, empirical observation, and faith.

Over the ages, reason has had a difficult road to travel. There have been numerous obstacles and counterforces: the reign of totalitarianism rather than democracy, the encouragement of obedience rather than independent thinking, the personal security found in superstition and magic, the unwillingness of people to engage in genuine dialogue, the insistence on being right at all costs, the belief that there is

*In Plato's *Theaetutus*

only one path to truth, the lack of openness to different points of view, and the use of manipulation rather than rational persuasion. Yet, in spite of these obstacles and counterforces, reason is still manifest in the lives of many.

Reason is especially manifest in the lives of the great philosophers. Perhaps the best way to answer the question, What is reason? is by examining the lives of the great philosophers. How do their lives differ from those whose center of gravity lies in daily life, science, or religion? By studying the lives of such notable personages as Socrates, Plato, Aristotle, Spinoza, Hume, Kant, Jaspers, and others, we can understand the life of reason.

Each of these named philosophers was unique and original in his philosophizing. This is what distinguished him as a great philosopher. Yet, as a group, they appear to have a common way—the life of reason.

Reason is a striving for unity in one's thinking. Each thinking person is bombarded with multitudinous facts and ideas. Often these elements of thought are diffuse and contradictory. Reason endeavors to consolidate these disparate facts and ideas into a meaningful whole.

Reason is constantly on the move. It questions, tests, and answers. And the answers often are considered to be only tentative—to be revised as better answers evolve. Reason advances, moves to a plateau, and then advances to a higher plateau. This steadfast movement is its very nature.

Reason subjects itself to criticism. Never quite complete, reason is constantly achieving ever-closer approximations of truth. Persons of reason will thus search out those who will challenge and disagree. And even unjustified criticism may be of value.

Reason assumes that there is no monopoly of truth. No individual or group exclusively possesses truth. Truth is available to all of us—regardless of our professional, political, or religious leanings.

Reason is the connecting link between all humans. How do we make contact with those individuals of different historical origins, who may speak a different language, and who may even be our adversaries? This contact can come about through reason. If two parties are willing to make a genuine commitment to use reason in working through their differences, they probably can arrive at mutually agreeable solutions. Occasionally, we may find that there are unresolvable differences in mental models, but without reason, all is lost.

These few salient attributes of reason personify the great philosophers. This common ground allows them to engage in authentic dialogue in their mutual search for truth.

In our quest for understanding the nature of reason, these great philosophers help form our mental models. Studying and reflecting on the life of a single philosopher, say, Socrates, helps us achieve a fair understanding of the life of reason. The same holds true for Spinoza or any great philosopher.

Integrating these various mental models across the people who hold them and value them offers us a paradigm—philosophy as a way of life. Jaspers refers to this as philosophical faith. And this paradigm is just as noble and potent as those of science and religion.

Now the question: Where is truth? As the connecting link between all persons, reason leads to truth-through-communication. In genuine dialogue between two persons, truth is both discovered and created. Witness the Gestalt truism that the whole is indeed greater than the sum of its parts.

Reason thus is an indispensable adjunct to the other three paths to truth: experience, observation, and faith. In everyday life of experience, we would be severely handicapped without the opportunity or willingness to reflect on our experience. In science, the researcher would be unable to make sense out of collected data without the use of reason. And in religion, we would find people possessed by irrational, rather than rational, faith. Indeed, reason essentially supplements each of these paths to truth. Without reason, each would founder.

All homage and respect aside, reason also has its limitation: reason provides process without content. Rather than a criticism of reason, this is simply an acknowledgement of what it is in its purity. While reason can provide a powerful means of analysis and synthesis, we must find content from experience, observation, and faith. Thus, reason is an essential apse of the Temple of Wisdom, but it is not the total temple.

* * * *

We began this chapter with the question, What can we know? This basic question posed by Kant demarcates the field of epistemology, a branch of philosophy that investigates the origin, nature, methods, and limits of human knowledge.

An answer to this fundamental question is provided by the Temple of Wisdom. With the atrium of the temple representing mental models, the apses represent four distinct paths to truth: experience, observation, faith, and reason. Wisdom is defined by the total temple. Remove any chamber and wisdom is constricted. Thus, the way to wisdom is to locate one's center of gravity in the atrium and to master the four paths to truth represented by the apses.

The Temple of Wisdom mirrors the Temple of Humanity. It provides a new understanding of truth.

The Temple of Wisdom, which recognizes both objective truth and subjective truth, elucidates four ways of validating truth:

- Experience: satisfying and practical consequences;
- Observation: compelling certainty of the facts;

- Faith: commitment to valued ends;
- Reason: truth-through-communication.

Thus, a distinct path to truth is found in each of the four apses of the temple. We can grasp truth by grasping it in each mode. Each mode of truth must maintain its integrity; we should allow each mode to grow. No single apse provides total truth and no single apse can claim a monopoly of truth. And importantly, one mode of truth should not interfere with another mode.

The Temple of Wisdom beckons all of us to break out of our shells. Finding our center of gravity in the atrium, we can become open to truth. As we view truth in a perpetual state of becoming, we realize that truth is both discovered and created. The important thing is to stay committed to the *whole* of truth. This is the way to wisdom.

Viewing truth through the lens of the Temple of Wisdom has profound implications for realizing a global ethic. By understanding the nature of mental models and paradigms, we come to appreciate the truths of people of different origins and different backgrounds. By grasping truth in each of the four modes, we realize the importance of all four world views—daily life, science, religion, and philosophy—in creating a global ethic. And by residing in the atrium, we understand how we can join with others in a mutual quest for ever higher truths. The real beauty of the temple is that it is open to all of humankind, from Scotland to South Africa to Bangladesh.

The challenge for leaders in the world community is to live a life of total dedication to the truth, to the *whole* of truth. And this commitment cannot be confined to the intellectual domain; it requires congruence between words and deeds.

V

THE GOOD LIFE

It is not a trivial question, Socrates said: What we are talking about is how one should live. Once constituted in that way, it very naturally moves from the question, asked by anybody, "how should I live?" to the question "how should anybody live?" That seems to ask for the reasons we all share for living one way rather than another. It seems to ask for the conditions of *the good life*—the right life, perhaps, for human beings as such.

BERNARD WILLIAMS
Ethics and the Limits of Philosophy

This quotation from Bernard Williams sets the stage for the present chapter. We are addressing essentially the same question that Socrates directed his attention to more than two millennia ago: What is the good life? And it is much broader than simply, What is the good life for you and me? But rather, What is the good life for humanity at large?

Let's frame the question by focusing on human values, specifically the personal values that characterize the good life. Yes, we find significant differences in values from one culture to another, as well as from one subculture to another. And, yes, we witness significant differences in values from one family to another, as well as from one individual to another. Given these vast differences in values, is it reasonable to expect that we can identify universal values, values that are common to humanity at large?

THE QUEST FOR UNIVERSAL VALUES

We can point to three specific works that attempt to identify universal values and ponder their appropriateness for a global ethic.

Rushworth Kidder, president of the Institute for Global Ethics, searched for an answer to this question: What core values must we uphold if humanity is to survive and prosper in an increasingly complex and fragile world? He traveled the world to interview leading thinkers, artists, writers, educators, business people, and religious and political leaders. Kidder asked each person the same question: "If you could develop a global code of ethics, what would it be?" Based on twenty-four interviews, he identified eight universal values that he considered basic to the moral conditions for a sustainable twenty-first century. They are love, truthfulness, fairness, freedom, unity, tolerance, responsibility, and respect for life. These findings are reported in his book *Shared Values for a Troubled World*.

The Parliament of the World's Religions, meeting in Chicago in 1993, involved respected leaders from all the world's major faiths. The interfaith declaration included a commitment to these guiding principles: (1) No new global order without a new global ethic; (2) Every human being must be treated humanely; (3) A culture of non-violence and respect for life; (4) A culture of solidarity and a just economic order; (5) A culture of tolerance and a life of truthfulness; and (6) A culture of equal rights and partnership between men and women. Within these guiding principles, we can identify several core values: treating others humanely, respect for life, unity, tolerance, truthfulness, and equal rights.

In the third work, *The Moral Sense*, James Q. Wilson, professor at UCLA, maintains that there is a universal moral sense. Based on considerable supportive research, Wilson identified four "universal sentiments": (1) *sympathy*: the capacity for and inclination to imagine the feelings of others; (2) *fairness*: equity, reciprocity, and impartiality; (3) *self-control*: the ability to restrain impulses for immediate pleasure in the light of higher values; and (4) *duty*: being faithful to obligations. Wilson found that these four sentiments were found in practically every culture of the world.

All three sources include both societal values and personal values. In this chapter, which is on the good life, we will concentrate on personal values. The final chapter will focus on societal values.

THE TEMPLE OF GOODNESS

In our quest for universal values, we will once again draw upon the Temple of Humanity for guidance. The Temple of Goodness, shown on the following page, mirrors the Temple of Humanity.

Lining up corresponding chambers of the two temples, we get this alignment:

- Humanitas: Integrity
- Daily Life: Contribution
- Philosophy: Communication
- Religion: Compassion
- Science: Cooperation*

These five core values are defined as follows:

- Integrity: living by a set of moral principles
- Contribution: making a difference, adding value to the human enterprise
- Communication: engaging in genuine dialogue
- Compassion: demonstrating an active concern for the well-being of others
- Cooperation: working with others to achieve a common goal

The good life is exemplified by these five core values. And this affirmation holds true for any culture, for any ethnic group, or for any religion. These core values are truly universal. They are framed in response to Socrates' question: What are the conditions of the good life for human beings as such?

---

*When we link science and cooperation, we are referring to the scientific community rather than to science *per se*.

The Temple of Goodness

To appreciate the importance of each of the five core values, consider what a given individual would be like if he or she were lacking any one of the values. What if a given individual manifested any four of the values but completely lacked the fifth. If the missing value, for example, was integrity, the individual could not be trusted. If the missing value was contribution, the individual would add no real value to the human enterprise. If the missing value was communication, the individual would be unable to relate to others. If the missing value was compassion, the individual would have no genuine concern for the welfare of others. And if the missing value was cooperation, the individual would not be able to function on a team. Indeed, each of the five values is essential to the whole.

Proposing these five core values as essential for the good life does not mean that the set of five is all-inclusive. Certainly there are other important values to consider, even though they would vary from culture to culture. But these five core values appear to constitute *a bare minimum* of what is necessary to define the good life—from Scotland to South Africa to Bangladesh.

INTEGRITY

The importance of integrity in everyday affairs is clearly pointed up in extensive research by James Kouzes and Barry Posner, professors at Santa Clara University. In two companion books, *The Leadership Challenge* and *Credibility*, the two authors describe their research and their findings. Several thousand respondents were asked to select from a list of twenty attributes those that they looked for and admired in their leaders. In every survey, the number one attribute most admired was *honest* (followed by competent, forward-looking, and inspiring). They also asked respondents to select the attributes that they looked for and admired in their colleagues and peers. Again, *honest* (followed by competent, dependable, and cooperative) topped the list.

Given the importance of honesty in human relationships, why is it that we find so many people behaving dishonestly? Why is it that so many people fail to live up to basic standards of integrity?

There no doubt are a number of possible answers to the question, but one reason in particular is especially noteworthy. Large numbers of people have been seduced by Machiavelli into believing that the end justifies the means: If the end is good, then any means—questionable or not—can justifiably be used to achieve the end.

Believing that the end justifies the means leads to rationalization. Given that the end is praiseworthy, it is then easy to make questionable means seem legitimate. We hear people say: "Well, everyone else is doing it." . . . "If we don't do it, someone else will." . . . "What we are doing is not nearly so bad as what they are doing." . . . "We will do it just this one time." . . . and on and on.

After such rationalization over a period of time, some people suffer the same fate as the boiled frog. Perhaps you know the story. If you place a frog in a bucket of hot water, it will jump out immediately. But take the same frog and place it in a bucket of cold water and heat the water slowly until it reaches the boiling point. There is something about frogs that allows their bodies to adjust to gradually increasing temperatures without receiving a danger signal. So you get a boiled frog. This happens to humans as a consequence of their repeated rationalizations and questionable decisions and deeds.

To avoid the fate of the frog, we must realize that integrity is the centerpiece of the Temple of Goodness, without which there would be no temple. The atrium "brings everything together."

Accordingly, we offer the following guiding principles for living a life of integrity. These principles, being derived from the religions and philosophies of the world, should hold true for any culture of the world.

Understand that human relationships are based upon trust. All genuine human relationships—husband and wife, business partners, employer and employee, friends—are based upon trust. Without trust there can be no genuine relationship. And trust grows out of honesty and integrity. It takes time to build this trust but only a moment to lose it.

Guide your life by a set of ethical principles. Decide on a set of ethical principles that will guide your life and then live by these principles. And there should not be one set of ethics for home and a different set for work. A unified life is guided by a single set of ethical principles.

View integrity as an end in itself. Some people behave ethically to achieve some "higher" goal, say, a business contract, employment, or in seeking admiration of others. This is myopic thinking. A life of virtue is an end in itself; it is not a means to some higher end.

Understand that the goal and the road leading to the goal must be in harmony. It is so easy to fall into the Machiavellian trap of rationalizing that the end justifies the means. But if the means is not in harmony with the goal, we will miss the goal, and the means will become the goal. This is the fate of the boiled frog.

Live for the long haul. One can easily succumb to acting on impulse for immediate pleasure or gratification. The wise person, even though tempted by the impulse, will reflect on the likely consequences of the action. And if the consequences are likely to be negative, the impulse will be suppressed. Long-term desires will override the short-term desires.

Treat others the way you would like to be treated. As shown on the following page, some version of the Golden Rule has been a core principle for each of the major world religions and philosophies. It is truly universal.

Be an active member of the group, but do not let that prevent you from standing up for what you think is right. Peer pressure for either a teen-ager or an adult can be formidable. Most people want to be accepted by their peers. But there comes a time when one must pull away from the group

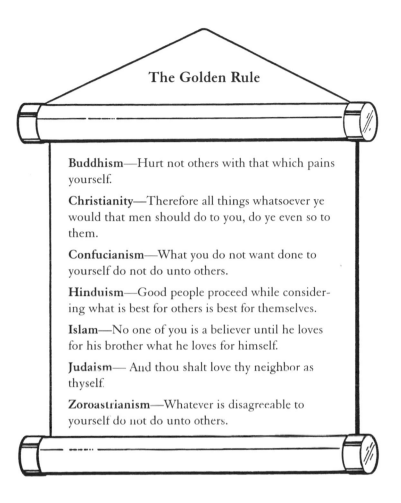

The Golden Rule

Buddhism—Hurt not others with that which pains yourself.

Christianity—Therefore all things whatsoever ye would that men should do to you, do ye even so to them.

Confucianism—What you do not want done to yourself do not do unto others.

Hinduism—Good people proceed while considering what is best for others is best for themselves.

Islam—No one of you is a believer until he loves for his brother what he loves for himself.

Judaism— And thou shalt love thy neighbor as thyself.

Zoroastrianism—Whatever is disagreeable to yourself do not do unto others.

and do what he or she thinks is the right thing to do—even if it means possible condemnation and rejection by the group.

Say "No" to anything that goes against what you believe is right. Suppose that your manager or someone in a higher position of authority in your organization instructs you to do something that you believe is unethical. Given your desire for job security, you might find yourself in a difficult predicament. But for your own personal security, try to persuade the manager or person in authority to do what is right. And if this fails, you must be able to walk away from it.

Admit your mistakes and then correct them. All of us make mistakes. Some find it extremely difficult to admit to others that they have made a mistake. But others admit their mistakes and then do whatever is necessary to correct them. The latter are more likely to gain the respect of others.

Have the courage to be. Your principles of ethics should be an integral part of the center core that guides your life. Often peripheral desires will oppose the center core. The "courage to be" means that you hold onto the center core, in spite of threats, even if it means sacrificing certain peripheral desires.

These guiding principles are not rules. They are heuristic, not algorithmic. Thus, they are intended for broad guidance. When faced with an ethical dilemma, each person must confront the situation, reflect on the appropriate principles, and then adapt them to the particular situation. In the final analysis, each person must be guided by his or her own conscience. And has been noted before, a clear conscience is the best pillow.

As a final point of consideration, here are words of the former president of the University of Notre Dame, Father Theodore Hesburgh:

> My basic principle is that you don't make decisions because they are easy, you don't make them because they are cheap, you don't make them because they are popular; you make them because they are right.*

---

*In *What Works for Me,* by Tom Horton.

CONTRIBUTION

The good life is more than "being good." It also includes "doing good." The world has given you much. What will you give back to the world? What will be your contribution to a better world?

Albert Schweitzer, in his book *Out of My Life and Thought*, provides a context:

> But however much concerned I was at the problem of the misery in the world, I never let myself get lost in broodings over it; I always held firmly to the thought that each one of us can do a little to bring some portion of it to an end.

Your daily life is rich with possibilities for making significant contributions. Among your possible contributions to making this a better world, consider the following guidelines.

Write an epitaph for yourself. This idea has been proposed in different forms, such as:

- Assume that you are retiring after many years of service in your job. At your retirement dinner what would you want the master of ceremonies to say?

- Assume that you have died. What would you want your family and friends to say?

By writing an epitaph for yourself, one that describes what you have contributed to make this a better world, you can create a vision for yourself, in terms of your desired future contributions.

Frame a "zone of contribution." You are limited in how much you can do in one lifetime. Because there are so many possibilities, you must set some priorities. Based upon the needs of others and your own interests and talents, identify a sphere where you can make the greatest contribution. Then persevere in applying your own talents to this particular sphere. But don't let the zone or limits of your sphere of contribution preclude you from other needs that might arise. Be concentrated but not *too* concentrated.

"Model the change that you would like to see in the world." In these words of wisdom, Mahatma Gandhi offered profound advice: reflect on what you think would be a better world and what changes would be required to bring this idea of a better world into being. Then you yourself *model the change*. Obviously this is easy to propose but difficult to do. But even a moderate amount of success will move theory into practice.

There are times for appropriate rebellion. Each person must decide if he or she will be an active change agent in building a better world or a mere spectator of an interesting scene. If it is the former, then there will be occasions when one must take a stand against dehumanizing events and forces. And one does not have to search far and wide to find these dehumanizing events and forces; they abound all around us. If we want to be more than mere spectators, we must act. Remember Seneca's challenge to all people of good will: "We cannot eliminate evil from the world, but we can prevent its victory."

The test is in the deed. There are some who might argue that the supreme test is found in faith: commitment and devotion to a particular religious creed. Without questioning the value of such faith, the ultimate test is found in the deed: What real contribution was made by the individual to help make this a better world?

The vast majority of contributions are made through small deeds. Some people wait for the eye-catching opportunity that allows them to make an earth-shaking contribution. An entire lifetime can go by waiting for such an opportunity.

But each day there are numerous opportunities for contributing through small deeds. And the aggregate of these small deeds over a lifetime makes a full and significant life.

In sum, be reminded that your potential for contribution is as broad as the Temple of Goodness and is fulfilled through your everyday deeds. Perhaps there will be few external rewards for these deeds. But the real reward comes from personal satisfaction received for contributing to a better world.

COMMUNICATION

The root word of "communication" is "commune." To commune means "to share"—to share our selves.

Interpersonal communication is so common, it often is taken for granted. We fail to appreciate its complexity and subtleties. One person attempts to translate some thoughts into verbal symbols; the receiver attempts to understand the verbal symbols and integrate them into thought. Beyond the words themselves, tone of voice and body language also convey information. Even when two persons try their best to communicate effectively, misunderstandings inevitably arise. Imagine the complexities when one or both of the parties are deceptive or manipulative.

Most interpersonal communication lacks genuine dialogue. People talk, but they don't say what they mean. People talk, but they don't express their inner thoughts and feelings. People talk, but they don't listen. Even with familiar words, communication fails.

Martin Buber, the philosopher of dialogue, identifies three distinctly different types of communication. First, there is monologue: one-way communication in which there is a sender but no receiver. Second, there is technical communication: two-way communication that involves the exchange of data and information. And third, there is dialogue: honest and open communication with the intention of establishing a living mutual relation. Unfortunately, the prevailing forms of communication for most people are monologue and technical communication. We see few instances of genuine dialogue.

Emil Fackenheim elucidates Buber's meaning of dialogue by contrasting the I-It relation and the I-Thou relation:

> While the I-It relation is necessarily abstract, the I-Thou relationship cannot be abstract. The partners communicate not this or that, but themselves; that is, they must *be in* the communication. Further—since the relation of dialogue is mutual—they must be in a state of openness to the other, that is, to this other at *this* time and in *this* place. Hence both the I and the Thou of every genuine dialogue are irreplaceable. Every dialogue is unique.*

Let's clarify the meaning of dialogue by contrasting it to its polar opposite: Machiavellianism. In the still popular book, *The Prince*, the well-known political writer of the sixteenth century, Niccolò Machiavelli, proposed to Prince Lorenzo a form of communication that is shrouded in insincerity and deception. Its intention is to achieve one's own personal end by manipulation. The end justifies the means. Dialogue, on the other hand, is grounded in sincerity and honesty. Its intention is the establishment of a living mutual relation. Contrast the quest for victory with the quest for mutual understanding.

In these two forms of communication, both the ends and the means are radically different. And with respect to developing a trusting relationship, the outcomes are radically different.

***The principal requirement for dialogue is authenticity*.** Authenticity means a congruence between the inner self and the outer self. Everyone carries these two selves: the inner self,

---

*In *The Philosophy of Martin Buber*, edited by Schilpp and Friedman.

which is known only to the possessor, and the outer self, which is witnessed by others. An individual is authentic to the extent that these two selves are in harmony. In the words of Abraham Maslow: "Phoniness is reduced toward the zero point." The *sine qua non* for dialogue is authenticity.

The two partners in dialogue are engaged in a quest for mutual understanding. In a debate, each participant is attempting to defeat the other, to achieve victory over the opponent, literally to "beat down." Unfortunately, even casual discussions between friends frequently turn into a debate. Dialogue is radically different. Here, the goal is to collaborate with the partner in a quest for mutual understanding. This is a different goal as well as a different attitude.

The two partners show genuine respect for each other. Even if the two partners disagree strongly in their views on specific issues, they nevertheless respect each other as a person of value. Each genuinely respects the otherness of the partner.

Both participants in dialogue are "fully present." Each fully concentrates on the exchange. Each is physically, mentally, and spiritually immersed in the dialogue.

Both participants are active listeners. A basic requirement of dialogue is listening, and it must be active listening. It is listening with understanding.

Both participants are spontaneous and unrehearsed. A rigid agenda can squelch dialogue because the presenter tries to cover all points in a prearranged order. In dialogue, both persons are spontaneous.

The participants share their mental models. They openly discuss the models themselves, the underlying assumptions of the models, and how they arrived at the models. Challenges are welcome.

The participants avoid premature evaluation. Whenever someone first proposes an idea, it seems only natural to classify it as either "good" or "bad." But in dialogue, each party attempts to fully understand an idea—by continuing to question and explore—before evaluating the idea.

Each helps the other to clarify his or her thoughts. Rather than put the partner on the defensive in trying to justify a preliminary idea, assistance is provided in clarifying the idea. Each person becomes clearer in his or her own thinking through the aid of the partner.

Both partners keep an open mind to opposing views and are willing to alter their views as new truths are uncovered. As Peter Senge says, "Larger understandings emerge by holding one's own point of view gently." This is quite different from the "I am right and you are wrong" attitude. Certainly the person engaged in dialogue is able to take a stand—but only after all reasonable avenues have been explored, understood, and assimilated.

Reflecting on these basic guidelines for dialogue, one might ask: "Aren't they just good common sense?" Yes. But then we ask: "If they are just common sense, why aren't they commonly applied in everyday affairs?"

By internalizing these basic guidelines, we make a genuine commitment to living a life of dialogue. The result will be enhanced interpersonal relationships and enhanced learning.

> When unity of self and others is experienced and communication reaches a heightened, personal meaning, life is being lived at a peak level. At times it seems unbelievable, almost beyond reach, but when it happens it is something of awesome beauty.
>
> —Clark Moustakes, *Loneliness and Love*

COMPASSION

I recall reading years ago about a woman whose actions belied her words. In the late 1800s, this woman reportedly had established a reputation for giving stimulating lectures to large audiences. The common theme of her lectures was her "love of mankind." On one especially cold winter night she was lecturing with great fervor on her love of mankind, but *she left her coachman out in the cold and he almost froze to death.* Now, many years later, I still carry in my head this vivid image: a woman in a warm lecture hall, lecturing with great passion on her love of mankind, while being oblivious to the plight of her coachman. Something seems to be terribly amiss.

People today would describe this woman lecturer as someone who does not "walk the talk": her actions are not consistent with her words. And certainly she is not the only person who has been guilty of this incongruity.

The compassionate person "walks the talk" and has a strong feeling for the condition of others, which is translated into deeds.

Compassion is *the active concern for the well-being of others.* *Well-being* means a favorable condition of existence. *Being concerned* means genuine interest in the condition of existence of others. Being *actively concerned* means to give of yourself through deeds in enhancing the condition of existence of others.

Compassion is best exemplified in what the psychologist Carl Rogers called "the helping relationship." As the leading exponent of nondirective therapy, Rogers devoted most of his adult life—as both a practitioner and a writer— to the subject of the helping relationship.

Rogers based his theory and practice on this premise:

> If I can provide a certain type of relationship, the other person will discover within himself the capacity to use the relationship for growth, and change and personal development will occur.

The key point is the relationship between the helper and the person being helped. It is the relationship itself that helps the other grow and develop. This nondirective approach stands in sharp contrast to a directive approach in which the helper gives instruction and advice to the person being helped. A large body of research lends considerable support to the nondirective approach espoused by Rogers.

In his popular book, *On Becoming a Person*, Rogers offers abundant practical guidelines for providing a helping relationship. These guidelines are not intended simply for professional psychotherapists; they are useful for ordinary people who desire to help others who may be in a state of despair. This might include a family member, a friend, a colleague at work, or even a stranger. It should prove beneficial to reflect on these guidelines and then employ them as appropriate when the situation arises.

Begin where the person is. A person comes to you seeking your aid and comfort. It's easy to begin with some type of normative model or ideal type of where you think the person *should be*. This approach may be mentally stimulating for you, but will be of no value for the person in need. The only logical point of departure is to begin where that person *is*, not where you think he or she *should be*. The "ought" must be suspended in favor of the concrete reality of the moment. And this reality has a threefold nature: the reality of the person in need, your own reality, and the reality of the relationship.

Accept the otherness of the person. The person being helped may very well differ from you in many respects. Be tolerant of the differences. And tolerance does not mean a patronizing tolerance. Not at all. It means accepting and showing a genuine respect for the differences between you and the person being helped.

Confirm the other as a person. To confirm means to acknowledge with definite assurance that you accept the person being helped, as an end and not as a means. Accept and confirm the person as a valuable being in his or her own right, in his or her own uniqueness.

Listen with empathy. The ladder of listening has three rungs: listening, active listening, and empathic listening. The third rung depends on the other two, but the first and second could take place without the third. Empathic listening means to listen actively and to truly try to comprehend the situation from the other person's perspective. You are trying to put yourself in that person's skin, so to speak, and feel the situation from his or her perspective.

Keep the relationship free of judgment and evaluation. In responding to the other person's statements, it seems very natural to say, "That's good" or "That's not so good." In the helping relationship, this tendency must be checked. If the judgment comes across as being either positive or negative, this puts you in the role of judge, that is, a superior-subordinate relationship. It also may suggest that you are attempting to calibrate the other person's mental models against your own, implying that yours should serve as the standard. Through your active listening, show that you understand what the person is saying without overtly judging or evaluating the merit of what is being said.

Be genuine in the relationship. This is no place for facades and phoniness. Be honest. Be sincere. Be genuine. These are crucial in establishing a trusting relationship between you and the person being helped.

Open channels that allow the other person to communicate thoughts and feelings. By confirming the person being helped and by listening with understanding, you create a climate that allows the person to reveal his or her thoughts and feelings. By being authentic, the other person can feel sufficiently secure to be authentic with you.

Don't rush in to "fix things." Many of us like to think that we are good problem solvers. Thus, when someone comes to us with a problem, we want to propose a solution. Resist the temptation. If we don't really understand the problem, we are likely to offer a solution that is not appropriate. Maybe the person in need should be the one who generates the solution. And maybe the person in need did not even want or expect a recommended solution, but only someone who would listen.

Meet the person as one who is in the process of becoming. We can confirm the person in need as he or she now is. Or we can confirm the person as what he or she might become. But even better: We can confirm the person as one who is in the process of becoming. The first two views are static and the third is dynamic. Your role as a facilitator should be to assist the person in the process of becoming.

Allow the person to grow in his or her own fashion. You may have a mental model of what you think the person in need should become as well as how the person should get there. There are two reasons *not* to impose your favorite mental model on the other person: first, it may be an inappropriate mental model for this person; and second, you will have prevented the person from developing his or her own mental model for growth. As the old adage goes: "Rather than give others a fish, it is better to teach them how to fish."

These guidelines capture the essence of Carl Rogers' views on nondirective counseling, which stands in sharp contrast to the directive approach. The latter approach can best be described as *controlling*: prescribing a course of action for the person in need. The nondirective approach, on the other hand, can best be described as *empowering*: enabling others to act by being a facilitator in their growth and development.

In the Synopsis we defined leadership as "influencing the thoughts, feelings, and/or behavior of others." Helping relationships provide the leader an opportunity to realize all three of these facets of leadership.

In summary, consider what Emily Dickinson* wrote:

> If I can stop one heart from breaking,
>   I shall not live in vain;
> If I can ease one life the aching,
>   Or cool one pain,
> Or help one lonely person
>   Into happiness again
> I shall not live in vain.

COOPERATION

In surveys conducted by James Kouzes and Barry Posner, they asked respondents to indicate what they admired most in their superiors and also in their associates. One attribute consistently selected was *cooperative* (along with honest, competent, and dependable). Most people surveyed want to work with associates who are cooperative. This is not surprising.

What is "cooperation"? Martin Buber, in *The Legend of the Baal-Shem*, provides an illustration:

> This is said in parable, "If a man sings and cannot lift his voice and another comes to help him and begins to sing, then this one too can now lift his voice. And that is the secret of cooperation."

---

*In *Poems That Touch the Heart*, compiled by A. L. Alexander.

Cooperation is an act of working together for a common purpose. This is essentially the definition for a team: two or more individuals working collaboratively to achieve a common goal. Thus, we can better understand cooperation by examining teamwork, and especially the attributes of a good team member.

There are numerous opportunities for being a member of a team: for example, the family, the organizational work unit, a project team, a political fund-raising committee, a neighborhood task force, and on and on. The opportunity arises whenever two or more people find themselves together to achieve a common goal. Teams may or may not have a formal leader.

Examining cooperation, we need to ask: What are the attributes of a good team member? From research and observation, we know that being a good team member is a learnable skill. But it requires commitment and practice.

Guidelines for being a good team member are presented below. These guidelines should enhance one's ability to be an effective team member.

Understand the importance of synergy. Synergy means that the whole is greater than the sum of its parts. So when two or more people work collaboratively, they can and often do achieve more than if they work independently. The team members will learn more and they will produce collective work-products that are better than what they would have produced had they worked independently.

Add value to the team. Every team member can contribute something unique and of value to the team. This might involve being a team leader . . . an assistant to the team leader . . . a facilitator . . . a source of information . . . a thoughtful questioner . . . a "sounding board" for the ideas of others . . . and on and on. What can your presence add to the team?

Keep the common goal in mind. As stated before, a team is a collection of individuals who are working collaboratively to achieve a common goal. Often a team will get sidetracked into peripheral issues and lose sight of the primary goal. A good team member helps keep the other team members on track by reminding them of the common goal.

Balance advocacy and inquiry. One of your roles on the team might be to advocate a certain position on a given issue, or inquire into the positions of others. The good team member does not assume one of these roles to the exclusion of the other, but achieves a balance of the two.

Listen with understanding. *Listen* to the other team members, *listen actively*, and *listen with understanding*. In doing so, you will gain a greater appreciation of their positions and how they arrived at their positions. Also, good listeners propagate more good listeners.

Hold your positions gently. One of the greatest deterrents to effective teamwork is the members' holding rigidly to their own positions and resisting all efforts by other team members to alter these positions. "Don't bother me with the facts; my mind is already made up." Rather than hold your position stubbornly, hold it "gently"; be willing to alter your position in the light of new evidence and rational argument.

Be willing to suspend your assumptions. This is undoubtedly one of the most difficult and challenging guidelines to implement. Every position on an issue is based upon assumptions, suppositions that are often taken for granted. If you are able to suspend your assumptions at least temporarily, you will be in a much better position to listen with understanding to the other team members and to keep an open mind to their positions.

Be willing to challenge the status quo. By accepting the status quo as the only reality, any team can "get into a rut." We hear team members respond to a new idea by saying, "But that is not the way we have always done it." What a deterrent to creativity! The good team member will be constantly searching for better ways to do things and will openly—and constructively—challenge the status quo.

Be willing to stand up for what is right. By focusing on a specific short-term goal, a team may lose sight of the larger picture. The team may fall in the trap of rationalizing that the end justifies the means. It might forget its core values. Whenever this happens, the good team member will interject appropriate reminders or will "raise a questioning finger" to remind the team of its higher level responsibilities.

Think win-win. Team members commonly get into the win-lose style of thinking. Whenever a conflict of ideas leads to a confrontation, we automatically assume that one individual must win and the other must lose. Transcend this attitude by focusing on a win-win solution. By exploring the merits of each position in the light of the team purpose, a team can arrive at a solution that is mutually acceptable to the different parties engaged in the confrontation.

Assume a leadership role when appropriate. A high-performance team allows and encourages different team members to assume a leadership role as the situation warrants. Different phases of a task or project will call for different kinds of knowledge and expertise. Whenever you are the most logical person to assume a leadership role, step forward.

Support decisions once they are made. One of the most dysfunctional acts that team members can take is to criticize team decisions subsequent to the team meeting. Whenever a decision is being made, that's when you should speak up and express your views. Sometimes the other team members will go along with your position and sometimes they will not. Regardless, it's an obligation to support the decision made by the team once it's made.

Help other team members succeed. You will have truly arrived as a good team member when you find yourself helping other team members succeed. Perhaps another team member is having difficulty carrying out his or her responsibility or achieving a particular goal. As you help, you will contribute to this team member's success as well as to the overall success of the team. Be prepared and be willing to offer your assistance to the other individual team members.

These several guidelines for being a good team member are not merely hypothetical or theoretical. Not at all. They have been tested and proven in the real-world crucible of cooperation and teamwork. But they are challenging—by no means easy to learn and apply. Once mastered, however, they will appear to be "just natural."

Many people never learn how to be a good team member, which is indeed a handicap both to themselves and to the various teams of which they are a part. Being a good team member is a learnable skill that practically anyone can master. Those who master this skill become more effective in their families, in their work units, in their team projects, in their volunteer activities—in any situation where two or more persons must work collaboratively to achieve a common goal. In the process of becoming better team members, these persons are likely to, first, gain a greater understanding of the meaning of cooperation, and second, become better human beings.

* * * * *

Now we can answer Socrates' question: What is the good life? The answer lies in the Temple of Goodness, which contains an atrium and four apses. The atrium represents integrity, and the four apses represent contribution, communication, compassion, and cooperation. These five core values capture the Humanitas view of the good life.

The five values function as a total set: They are interrelated and each is an essential element in the whole. This point is given credence by the root of the English word "good": "Ghedh" means to unite, join, to bring together. Thus, for one to achieve goodness, the five core values must be "brought together." And it should be noted that integrity, the value reflected by the atrium of the temple, has two meanings: (1) honesty and (2) the state of being whole.

Would the great spiritual leaders agree with this depiction of the good life? Suppose we were given the opportunity to meet with Buddha, Confucius, Mahatma Gandhi, Jesus, Lao-tzu, the Prophet Muhammad, and Moses, and asked them this question: Are you in general agreement with this description of the good life? I believe that they would agree, and I hold this belief because, in constructing the Temple of Goodness, I have drawn from their collective wisdom.

The challenge for leaders in the world community is to be truly committed to the good life. This means, in essence, to do good and to avoid evil. Such a life is achieved by doing what you can to enhance human flourishing and to avoid thwarting human flourishing—both your own and that of others.

VI

A GLOBAL COMMUNITY

When you see the earth from the moon, you don't see any divisions there of nations or states. This might be the symbol for the new mythology to come. This is the country that we are going to be celebrating. And these are the people that we are one with.

JOSEPH CAMPBELL
The Power of Myth

T he previous three chapters have addressed these questions: (1) What does it mean to be human? (2) What can we know? and (3) What should we do? We now come to the fourth question: What may we hope for? This final question to be addressed is equal in importance to the first three.

What is meant by "hope"? We can begin with a dictionary definition: desire with expectation of fulfillment. This desire can be either passive or active. Passive desire is wishful thinking for something—a fancy—but is found lacking in will and commitment to bring it into being. This type of desire may give us a warm feeling, but other than that, it does not bear fruit. Active desire, on the other hand, is a strong wish for something, and this strong wish is accompanied by will and commitment. This type of desire will bear fruit.

Our focus here is on *active* desire, *active* hope. This type of hope is so important that we are willing to commit ourselves to it, that is, commit our *selves* to it. While we realize that what is hoped for may not be realized in our lifetimes, we nevertheless will devote ourselves to pursuing this hope.

What goal would be so lofty that it would appeal to the hearts and minds of people around the world? What possible goal would be so worthy? This is the Humanitas answer: *We should hope for a global community*. This global community can be represented as a circle with a common center and a multitude of radii. The common center represents a shared vision and shared values, and the radii represent individual persons of all nationalities, all ethnic groups, and all religious faiths. We realize, of course, that such a hope might not be realized in our lifetimes, but we nevertheless should strive for it with all our might. And we should celebrate small victories along the way.

But before addressing the topic of a global community, let's clarify what we mean by community.

THE NATURE OF COMMUNITY

Martin Buber, in an essay titled "Comments on the Idea of Community," provides an illuminating metaphor for community:

> The real essence of community is undoubtedly to be found in the—manifest or hidden—fact that it has a center. The real origin of community is undoubtedly only to be understood by the fact that its members have a common relationship to the center superior to all other relations: the circle is drawn from the radii, not from the points of the periphery.

This communal circle has a center and numerous radii. The radii represent the many individual persons in the community, and the center represents what the members have in common, what holds them together. This metaphor captures the essence of community, which has as its root word *communitat*, which means "common." Without a common center, there can be no community.

What serves as the common center for genuine community? We know for certain that it is not a geographical boundary; it is not an entity established by law; nor is it necessarily a particular organization of people. No, not at all. Community is where community happens, without being mandated.

What makes community happen is a common center that appeals to the hearts and minds of the members. Finding the common center comes about through dialogue. This common center may be in the form of common concerns, a common goal, or common values—some or all of these combined. These are the intangibles—quite different from geographical boundaries, orders and edicts, and organization charts—but are the very stuff of community. These intangibles generate and maintain what we call community spirit.

History has shown that a common center can be found in a hamlet, in a village, in a city-state, and even in a nation. We now ask: Can we advance to the next rung on the ladder of social development and find a common center for the peoples of the world? The key will be dialogue.

THE TEMPLE OF HOPE

A fruitful initial step in translating a hope into an action is to create a vision that depicts the hope. A vision is a clear mental picture of a desired future. It serves as the lodestar and inspiration for our actions.

The Humanitas vision is found in the Temple of Hope, which is shown on the following page. The temple contains an atrium and four apses. With the atrium representing the global citizen, the four apses represent four societal values: rights and responsibilities, democracy, peace, and a common ethic.

The Temple of Hope, like the three previous temples, is a mirror of the Temple of Humanity. We find a reasonably good alignment between the two sets of chambers:

- Humanitas: The Global Citizen
- Daily Life: Rights and Responsibilities
- Science: Democracy
- Religion: Peace
- Philosophy: A Common Ethic

The Temple of Hope

The only pair that might raise a question in the reader's mind is science and democracy. Here we are referring to the scientific community rather than to science per se. Jacob Bronowski, in *Science and Human Values*, clarifies the linkage: "The society of scientists must be a democracy. It can keep alive and grow only by a constant tension between dissent and respect; between independence from the views of others, and tolerance for them." In essence, what the scientific community and the democratic community have in common is that the members "reason together."

Each chamber of the Temple of Hope is an integral part of the whole. The atrium (the global citizen) highlights the principal area of focus in building a global community. The south apse (rights and responsibilities) makes special note of what is *due to* all citizens and what is *due from* all citizens. The west apse (democracy) reflects the only form of government worthy of being established in a global community. The east apse (peace) represents the *sine qua non* of a global community. And the north apse (a common ethic) represents the conscience of a global community. All five chambers are essential to the building of a global community.

THE GLOBAL CITIZEN

Many world travelers "act globally and think locally." When people travel far and wide to distant countries—businesspeople and tourists alike—they tend to carry their own local cultures with them. The idea of what constitutes a good life, a good religion, a good culture is locked tightly in their mental models. Eric Hoffer would call these world travelers "True Believers." For them, there is only one way to truth and the good life—and that is *their* way.

These True Believers have petrified world views and are trapped within the shells of these world views. They come across as being culturally arrogant because they *are* culturally arrogant. They have the strange notion that, for some reason, their own culture is somehow superior to all others. These people contribute nothing to promote a global community. They detract.

In contrast to the True Believer, the global citizen "thinks globally and acts locally." The global citizen has a sense of oneness with humanity: all humans are brothers and sisters, members of the human community. This global orientation is then manifested at the local level in relations with individuals of diverse cultures and backgrounds. There is no need to travel far and wide to be a global citizen. Global citizenship is lived out in the everyday life of the local community.

Being a global citizen is an attitude, a frame of mind. It leads us to view ourselves as citizens of the world. No passports or formal documents are needed.

The central meaning of world citizenship is captured in a pamphlet on that subject published by the Bahá'í International Community:

> *World citizenship* begins with an acceptance of the oneness of the human family and the interconnectedness of the nations of "the earth, our home." While it encourages a sane and legitimate patriotism, it also insists upon a wider loyalty, a love of humanity as a whole. . . . Its hallmark is "unity in diversity."

To be a true global citizen, there are at least three basic requirements: maintaining a global orientation, holding to universal values, and mastering core learning disciplines. Each is an essential feature of the whole.

Global orientation means viewing oneself as a global citizen. This is an attitude, a disposition that helps form one's sense of identity. It is a feeling of oneness with humanity, a genuine feeling that one is a member of the human family. This attitude leads to an active concern for the well-being of the people of the world, regardless of their race, religion, or nationality. It promotes the idea that "We are all in this together; we are all on a common journey."

The universal values are those included in the Temple of Goodness: integrity, contribution, communication, compassion, and cooperation. To review: integrity means to live by a set of moral principles; contribution is "making a difference" in building a better world; communication is engaging in genuine dialogue; compassion is actively caring for the well-being of others; and cooperation is working with others to achieve a common goal. Any person who holds to and lives by these core universal values is welcomed into the global community.

The core learning disciplines represent the third requirement for global citizenship. Peter Senge, in his popular book, *The Fifth Discipline*, identifies these five core learning disciplines:

- *Systems Thinking:* a way of thinking about, and a language for describing and understanding, the forces and interrelationships that shape the behavior of systems.

- *Personal Mastery:* learning to expand our personal capacity to create the results we most desire.

- *Mental Models:* reflecting upon, clarifying, and improving our internal pictures of the world, and seeing how they shape our decisions and actions.

- *Shared Vision:* building a sense of commitment in a group, by developing shared images of the future we seek to create and the principles and guiding practices by which we hope to get there.

- *Team Learning:* transforming conversational and collective thinking skills, so that groups of people can reliably develop intelligence and ability greater than the sum of individual members' talents.

One who learns and masters these five core learning disciplines will be well suited for global citizenship. Systems thinking allows one to see the world as a whole, how the many variables interact, and where the high-leverage variables might be found. Personal mastery encourages one to be a lifelong learner and to keep expanding one's basic talents. Mental models allow an understanding of one's own internal pictures of the world and how to understand and appreciate the internal pictures of others. Shared vision highlights the need for the peoples of the world to hold a common mental picture of a desired future. And team learning helps one appreciate the importance of diversity if our collective intelligence is to be greater than the sum of the intelligence of the individual members. Each of these core learning disciplines is important individually, but when all five are functioning as an integrated set, we witness something of awesome beauty.

These three basic competencies are essential for global citizenship: maintaining a global orientation, holding to universal values, and mastering core learning disciplines. Internalizing only one or two of these requirements might qualify one for provisional citizenship in the global community. But internalizing all three would qualify one for full citizenship.

One might ask why the Global Citizen is in the atrium of the Temple of Hope. There is an important reason: it would seem that the global citizen is the high-leverage factor for building a global community. Certainly there are other entities that can make a substantial contribution, including the United Nations, national governments, the scientific community, the Council for a Parliament of the World's Religions, transnational corporations, and still others. These are institutions that can indeed promote and accelerate the movement. But in the final analysis, individual persons—in lands around the world—who see themselves as citizens of the world and who live out of this orientation will have a true and lasting effect.

No doubt, many people around the world already view themselves as global citizens. But just suppose that this number could be increased a hundredfold and then a thousandfold. It is unimaginable what might be accomplished in the building of a global community. What we would then witness would be a "community of communities."

Dag Hammarskjöld, the late Secretary-General of the United Nations, presented each person in the world this summons:

> Everybody today, with part of his being, belongs to one country, with its specific traditions and problems, while with

another part he has become a citizen of the world which no longer permits national isolation. Seen in this light there could not be any conflict between nationalism and internationalism, between the nation and the world.

RIGHTS AND RESPONSIBILITIES

Numerous documents supporting the concept of human rights are now in existence. A sample of standard-setting and implementation documents published by the United Nations carry these titles:

- Universal Declaration of Human Rights
- Declaration on the Granting of Independence to Colonial Countries and Peoples
- Convention on the Prevention and Punishment of the Crime of Genocide
- Declaration on Protection from Torture
- Convention Relating to the Status of Refugees
- Declaration on the Elimination of All Forms of Intolerance and of Discrimination Based on Religion or Belief
- International Covenant on Economic, Social, and Cultural Rights
- International Covenant on Civil and Political Rights
- International Convention on the Elimination of All Forms of Racial Discrimination
- International Convention on the Suppression and Punishment of the Crime of Apartheid
- Convention on the Elimination of All Forms of Discrimination against Women

- Convention on the Rights of the Child

- International Convention on the Protection of the Rights of All Migrant Workers and Their Families

- Convention Against Discrimination in Education

These particular titles have been selected to illustrate the breadth of the subject of human rights. One will find in these documents scores of specific human rights that have been affirmed by the United Nations. But affirmation and implementation are not always aligned.

Every nation appears to agree with the concept of human rights. But when it comes to actually delineating what those rights should be, we find no small amount of disagreement. Given the importance of national sovereignty, should one nation define human rights for another? Or should the United Nations define human rights for all nations—or at least for all member nations? This is the ongoing debate.

Let's consider this question: Are there certain universal human rights that apply to all people in all cultures at all times? An affirmative response leads to a second question: What are these specific human rights? And this then leads to still a third question: How are these specific human rights to be assured? These questions are of central importance in the development of a global ethic.

To the first question—Are there universal human rights?— the Humanitas answer is a resounding "Yes." Inasmuch as Humanitas is a global philosophy that cuts across national borders, cultures, and religions, it is grounded in the belief that there are indeed universal human rights and that these rights must be affirmed and actively supported.

To the second question—What are these specific human rights?—Humanitas also has an answer. But the answer is based on this premise: human rights cannot be separated from human responsibilities. The two are reciprocal. One without the other severely dampens human flourishing.

In the report, "Towards a Global Ethic," the Council for a Parliament of the World's Religions stresses the complementary nature of rights and responsibilities:

> Every individual has intrinsic dignity and inalienable rights, and each also has an inescapable responsibility for what she or he does and does not do. All our decisions and deeds, even our omissions and failures, have consequences.

Given this premise of the complementariness of rights and responsibilities, we are then in a position to elucidate a Humanitas view of human rights. We will do this through one basic proposition and two corollaries.

Basic proposition: *Everyone has the right to be a human being*. A carpenter has the right to be a carpenter. . . . A physician has the right to be a physician. . . . A member of a trade union has the right to be a member of that trade union. . . . A member of a particular religious faith has a right to be a member of that religious faith. . . . A parent has the right to be a parent. Given these basic human rights, it should follow that the most fundamental right of all is that everyone has the right to be a human being.

We can elucidate this right to be a human being in the light of our model of the fully functioning person. Our response to the question, What does it mean to be human?—was given in terms of the fully functioning person, one who has four requisite capabilities: coping, knowing, believing, and being. Thus, we would affirm that, to be a fully functioning person, everyone has the right to cope, the right to know, the right to believe, and the right to be. These are universal human rights.

First corollary: *Everyone has the responsibility to be a human being*. Greek comedy gives us a cogent line: "How delightful a thing a human being could be, if he were a human being." How true. Every human organism is born with the potential to be a human being. But by being inhuman, some never realize this potential.

Second corollary: *Anyone who does not assume the responsibility for being a human being will lose some of the rights associated with being a human being.* This corollary captures the essence of the social contract between the human community and each member of that community. The community affirms that each member has the right to be a human being, but if a member abuses that right—say, through lawlessness or unethical conduct—then he or she has forfeited the basic right proffered by the human community.

We then come to the third question in the series: How are universal human rights to be assured? Advocacy alone is not sufficient. Recognition of and compliance with human rights standards requires (1) human rights agreements among nations of the world with agreed-upon and enforceable penalties for violations, and/or (2) a strengthened United Nations with the authority to enforce human rights agreements. The assurance of human rights requires both advocacy and the authority of sanctions.

In sum, rights and responsibilities are an essential apse in the Temple of Hope. Without this apse, the temple would not be a temple.

DEMOCRACY

The west apse of the Temple of Hope represents democracy, which Mahatma Gandhi loved with a passion. He believed that "Democracy, disciplined and enlightened, is the finest thing in the world." But note carefully his qualifiers: disciplined and enlightened. He is not saying that any form of democracy is the finest thing in the world, but only that form that is disciplined and enlightened.

Winston Churchill was not as positive as Gandhi in his comments about democracy. Churchill was not joking when he remarked, "Democracy is the worst form of government in the world—except for all the other forms." Churchill was a realist. He was quite familiar with the sometimes negative concomitants of democracy: for example, elected leaders who are irresponsible and corrupt, an indifferent electorate, freedom without responsibility, and on and on. Even so, when comparing democracy with other forms of government, he was convinced that democracy was the best. Whenever we feel disenchanted with democracy because of its shortcomings, we should remind ourselves of this remark by Churchill.

The Humanitas position is that democracy is a universal human right. All citizens of a given community have a right to share in the political power of that community: by voting on political candidates and community-wide issues and by participating actively in community affairs.

It also is the Humanitas position that democracy is the only form of government worthy of being included in a global community. We say this for two principal reasons.

First, a democratic form of government will make the greatest contribution in helping its citizens become fully human. Citizens need freedom and opportunity to become fully functioning persons. Thus, they must be given the freedom to cope, the freedom to know, the freedom to believe, and the freedom to be. These freedoms are the hallmark of democracy.

Second, a democratic form of government will make the greatest contribution in helping the world become a global community. Given that a "disciplined and enlightened" world community would be far superior to a world government, democracy can show the way. When all nations of the world become democracies, we truly will achieve a worldwide "community of communities."

Consider the other principal forms of government now in existence around the world: socialism, communism, military, and monarchy. If we evaluate these forms of government along with democracy on the basis of the two stated criteria—helping citizens become fully human and helping to build a global community—there is no contest. Democracy wins hands down.

As we examine the contribution of democracy to building a global community, let's review some basics. The aggregate of these basics will provide a capsule summary of what is meant by democracy.

- The root word of democracy is *demos*, meaning the people; the people make the decisions. Democracy means government for, by, and of the people.

- Democracy is grounded in faith in the wisdom of the people. It assumes that, in the majority of cases, the people as a whole will make better decisions than a single ruler, that is, decisions that are better for the people as a whole.

- Democracy calls for a balancing of freedom and authority. Freedom without authority leads to anarchy; authority without freedom leads to totalitarianism; but the proper balance of freedom and authority leads to true democracy. Thus, what is promised by democracy is liberty within a framework of law.

- Democracy provides a system in which the people can reason together. Democracy assumes reason in the service of the common good. Through forums and public debates—guided by rationality—the citizenry and their elected representatives are expected to deal with the critical issues of the day.

- Democracy accepts and promotes a diversity of opinion. Only by allowing diverse opinions to be expressed—by majorities and minorities alike—will all positions be fairly represented. Here we can appreciate the advantage of a two-party system (or multi-party system) over a single-party system.

- Democracy promotes active citizen participation in the affairs of government. In his book, *To Have Or To Be?*, Erich Fromm makes a clear distinction between "spectator democracy" and "participative democracy." In the former, the citizenry may vote in the general elections, but, with regard to their participation in the affairs of government, that is pretty much the extent of it. In the latter, the citizens of the community are actively concerned about the affairs of the larger community, and their concern is expressed through action—actions that benefit the community as a whole.

- Democracy is an idea, a concept of government for, by, and of the people. But an idea is not a concrete reality. We can point to many nations that have embraced and established the democratic form of government, but we can point to none of them and say, "This is exactly what is meant by democracy." The ideal form of democracy is beyond our comprehension.

Given this brief review of the basics of democracy, we can now return to the question, What can we hope for? The Humanitas answer to the question is that we can hope that every nation in the world establishes a democratic form of government. This is our hope.

On a global scale, the democratic nations must help the others find their way. Tolerance, understanding, and patience will be required. And of utmost importance will be the acceptance of flexibility in the concept of democracy. No single nation has all the answers.

William O. Douglas, Associate Justice of the U.S. Supreme Court from 1939 to 1975, thought deeply about democracy and its evolutionary nature. In his essay "The Case for Democracy," he has this to say:

> Democracy, unlike refrigerators and steel mills, is not an exportable commodity. It is a way of life, contagious among those who have come to see its potential for the spirit and mind of men. It takes root slowly in new lands. It may take a long, long time for full flowering.

Douglas was a pragmatic idealist. As an idealist, he fully embraced the idea of all nations becoming democracies. As a pragmatist, he realized that such an achievement would be a herculean task. Even so, each small step toward the vision would be a small victory.

Understand and appreciate that democracy is not an end-state but an ongoing quest. The general idea of democracy we have in front of us makes us realize that there are many paths that can lead to democracy. So we must be patient: as past experience has clearly demonstrated, there will be failures and setbacks along the way. But in our promotion of a global community, it is essential that we—you and I—keep the idea of democracy alive and promote its "full flowering."

PEACE

Our spokesman for the east apse of the Temple of Hope is the Dutch humanist Desidereus Erasmus. In the book *The Praise of Folly*, Erasmus posed this question:

> Is not war the very root and matter of all famed enterprises? And yet what more foolish than to undertake it for I know

what trifles, especially when both parties are sure to lose more than they get in the bargain?

The question is just as relevant today as when *The Praise of Folly* was published in the year 1509. We continue to ask Why? Why? War is pure folly, and the majority of people in the world know that it is pure folly. Yet we continue to have wars. Why?

Actual warfare is such a tragedy, but so is the constant preparation for war. What the world witnesses is either warfare itself or the continual preparation for war. There seems to be no end. And the horrendous costs—in lives, suffering, heartbreak, as well as in currency. We can only ask Why? Why? Why?

A study of the history of warfare sheds some light. Obviously, warfare has an ambivalent nature: there is simultaneous repulsion and attraction. The repulsion is all-too-obvious: the deaths, the suffering, the agony. The other side of the equation is more subtle.

The attraction of warfare is the glory and valor. Read any book on great leaders and what will you find? There will be a small amount of space devoted to leaders in religion, education, business and industry, and science. But the greatest amount of space will be devoted to leaders in politics and the military. When people think of great leaders, they often think of military leaders who achieved greatness in battle.

When we talk with individuals who have served in battle during their lives, these war veterans might mention their careers, their families, and their travels. But the greatest animation is shown when they begin to describe their experiences in the military, and especially in battle. The time in battle was the high point in their lives. It is what Abraham Maslow would call a "peak experience."

I recall a conversation years ago with a U.S. Air Force pilot who had only two years remaining in his 20-year military career. His one principal desire at the time was to fly one more mission. For him, that would have been a peak experience.

I also recall reading some years ago an interview with an Arab paramilitary member. In the transcript of the interview, the interviewer continued to ask the interviewee what motivated him to make the great sacrifices and to expose himself to such great risks. Why did he do it? The bottom line was that engaging in paramilitary activities was far more exciting than tending sheep. And so it goes.

We are thus faced with the ambivalent nature of warfare: agony and sorrow on the one hand, and the glory and valor on the other. To achieve world peace—and what Immanuel Kant called "perpetual peace"—we must come to grips with this issue.

Almost a century ago, the philosopher William James proposed a profound solution to the problem of war. He is well known for his idea of the "moral equivalent":

> One hears of the mechanical equivalent of heat. What we now need to discover in the social realm is the moral equivalent of war: something heroic that will speak to men as universally as war does, and yet will be as compatible with their spiritual selves as war proved itself to be incompatible.*

Indeed, James was undoubtedly correct: we must find the moral equivalent of war, to provide the valor, the glory, and the challenge heretofore provided only by warfare. In addition, it should appeal to our spiritual selves. What might it be?

Humanitas says there is indeed a moral equivalent of war. It should appeal to the hearts and minds of people around the world. It offers the greatest challenge to the people of the world. And it has the potential for bringing about perpetual

---

*In *The Varieties of Religious Experience*.

peace. The moral equivalent of war is *building a global community*.

A global community would be one in which the peoples of the world would have a common center: a shared vision of a better world. And the peoples of the world would work collaboratively to make the vision a reality. Such an idea may have been too remote in William James's day. But today, it is a real possibility—and necessity.

In the Humanitas proposal for building a better world, we have now put four stakes into the ground. These were the first three: the idea of the global citizen, the promotion of universal rights and responsibilities, and the promotion of democracy throughout the world. And this is the fourth: achieving perpetual peace by building a global community. These four stakes are interconnected and mutually reinforcing. Collectively, they can help build a better world for all.

So as not to appear Utopian in our desire for a global community, we must acknowledge the inevitable obstacles. Can we expect large numbers of people around the world to be opposed to the idea of a global community? The answer is "absolutely yes." Can we expect some people to take stringent action to impede any movement toward a global community? Again, the answer is "absolutely yes." But even so—even with these inescapable obstacles—can we progress in building a global community? And the answer is a resounding "yes!" We can make this assertion with confidence because it is happening at this very hour.

There is so much that leaders in the world community can do to help build a global community. These are some possibilities:

- The United Nations can revitalize its position in "maintaining international peace and security, achieving international cooperation in solving international problems, and in promoting respect for human rights and for fundamental freedoms."

- The political leaders of the many nations can model the way by negotiating win-win solutions in resolving their differences.

- Religious leaders can continue the fine work of the Parliament of the World's Religions in drafting and promoting a global ethic.

- Educational leaders can incorporate the idea of a global community in the curricula of the schools and colleges.

- Leaders in the scientific community can initiate collaborative projects that will enhance quality of life for all peoples.

- Business leaders can actively support fair and equitable international trade agreements and then engage in fair and equitable trade.

- Leaders in the arts and literature can select themes associated with a global community.

- The media can play a major role by reporting small victories along the way.

These ideas for building a global community could significantly contribute to attaining perpetual peace. The cessation of war does not mean real peace. Real peace—perpetual peace—will be achieved only through building a global community.

William James was correct in his diagnosis: we must find the moral equivalent of war. And that moral equivalent is found in the vision of a global community. It is within our grasp.

If this vision can become a reality, then the world may someday witness Isaiah's prophecy:

> They shall beat their swords into plowshares, and their spears into pruning hooks; nation shall not lift up sword against nation, neither shall they learn war any more.*

A COMMON ETHIC

A journey to the north apse of the Temple of Hope will allow us to summarize the Humanitas philosophy. The theme is "a common ethic."

Leaders in the world community have begun to recognize the need for a global ethic. They understand the need for a set of moral principles for determining right and wrong, a set of core values that would be generally accepted by the peoples of the world. They pose this question: What are the universal values that will provide a moral compass?

Many of these leaders accept the following logic. Human flourishing on a global scale will depend heavily on building a global community, which will depend heavily on framing a generally acceptable global ethic. Going in reverse order: framing a global ethic will contribute substantially to building a global community, and building a global community will contribute substantially to human flourishing.

Thus, we should start at the beginning. By developing a global ethic, we can start a chain reaction that will eventually lead to a better world for all. And that is the aim of Humanitas.

The sociologist Robert Bellah helps clarify the need for a global ethic:

> I think it's a very exciting prospect to be facing a new millennium. And of course that raises all kinds of fears and hopes.

*Isaiah 2:4.

150

But to me the most critical question is how can we give interdependence—which is so obvious in connection with everything we do—a moral meaning? Interdependence without moral meaning is terrifying.*

There is great wisdom in what Bellah is saying. Consider, for example, the General Agreement on Tariffs and Trade (GATT), an ambitious world trade accord that involves more than 100 nations. When it was finally signed—after years of negotiation—there was celebration. But we must appreciate that it is only a written accord. There is indeed a printed document, and the leaders of the many nations did affix their signatures to the document. But what does it mean? Without a common ethic to go with the document, the trade agreement will be for naught. As Bellah correctly asserts, "Interdependence without moral meaning is terrifying."

A common ethic would be composed of a set of core moral principles mutually agreed upon by the peoples of the world. These moral principles would serve as guidelines for living in an interdependent world. While each individual nation and ethnic group would be expected to maintain its own individuality and its own cultural values, it nevertheless would be expected to abide by the core moral principles mutually agreed upon. This would be the common ethic.

A World View

In this ambitious undertaking of framing a global ethic, where do we begin? Each of the three principal world views—science, religion, and philosophy—can be expected to make a significant contribution. And we should not ignore the realities of daily life.

---

*In *A World of Ideas*, by Bill Moyers.

These several world views are the building blocks of the Temple of Humanity, which contains an atrium and four apses. With the atrium representing Humanitas and the four apses representing daily life, religion, science, and philosophy, we have a universal *Weltanschauung*, a universal world view. This *Weltanschauung* then serves as the broad framework for developing a global ethic.

A comprehensive global ethic calls for answers to four fundamental questions: (1) What does it mean to be human? (2) What can we know? (3) What should we do? and (4) What may we hope for?

What Does It Mean to be Human?

We can address this question either in terms of what humans *are* or in terms of what humans *can become*. The latter approach seems to be more fruitful.

Each human organism is born with the potential for being fully human, for being a fully functioning person. Some individuals do indeed achieve this potential and some do not. The failure to realize one's potential may be due to the individual's own lack of resolve or to external forces beyond the individual's control—or perhaps to a combination of the two.

The fully functioning person is depicted by the Temple of Human Potential, which is composed of an atrium and four apses. With the atrium representing the art of living, the four apses represent the art of coping, the art of knowing, the art of believing, and the art of being. The fully functioning person lives out of the total temple.

This model of the fully functioning person—what it means to be human—has two especially attractive features. First, it is valid for people throughout the world, from Scotland to South Africa to Bangladesh. And second, it can serve as the touchstone for evaluating the various institutions that are expected to serve their members, for example, governmental systems, educational systems, and religious organizations. If any one of these institutions does not help—or even hampers—individual members in their quest to become fully functioning persons, then that institution would be suspect.

What Can We Know?

The quest for truth is an unending quest for large numbers of people around the world. In this quest, some will take a firm hold of one aspect of truth and assume that it is the total truth. In contrast, the Humanitas philosophy is committed to a more encompassing view of truth.

This commitment leads to the construction of the Temple of Wisdom, which contains an atrium and four apses. With the atrium representing mental models, the four apses represent four modes of truth: experience, observation, faith, and reason.

A grasp of mental models helps one understand the meaning of truth. Mental models are representations of the world—assumptions and generalizations—that we carry in our heads. They link the subjective thinker and the thought object. With the thought object constituting reality, the mental model represents that reality. The essence of truth is found in the connection between the mental model and reality.

If people around the world would fully grasp the nature of mental models and paradigms, we would have a better world. We would witness greater mutual understanding, greater tolerance, and less cultural arrogance.

What Should We Do?

The quest for the good life has been of great concern to people around the world since the beginning of philosophy and the founding of the world's religions. Various answers can be found in the different religions, the different philosophies, and the different cultures.

The question of the good life was of great interest to Socrates. This early Greek philosopher sought an answer that would apply to people everywhere and at all times.

The Temple of Goodness provides an answer to Socrates' question. With the atrium representing integrity, the four apses represent contribution, communication, compassion, and cooperation. These five core values, collectively, capture the essence of the good life. And they are universal: they apply to people everywhere and at all times.

What May We Hope For?

This final question in the series helps define what we mean by a better world. It helps create the vision of what we would like to see the world become.

The Temple of Hope is composed of an atrium and four apses. With the atrium representing the global citizen, the four apses represent rights and responsibilities, democracy, peace, and a common ethic. These five chambers of the temple are interconnected and, collectively, can point the way to a better world.

The challenge for leaders in the world community is to help build this better world. To this end, accepting dual citizenship is a fundamental requirement. One can—and must—be both a citizen of his or her own country and a citizen of the world. The enlightened leader will realize that these two roles are not contradictory, but are complementary and mutually reinforcing.

* * * *

In closing, I would like to leave you with this thought:

One person can make a difference. *You* can make a difference. And you *will* make a difference when you adhere to a single standard of conduct, adopt a spirit of service, and act within a moral framework.

—Keshavan Nair
A Higher Standard of Leadership:
Lessons from the Life of Gandhi

APPENDIX

EXERCISES

These exercises will help you translate theory into practice. By reflecting on each question and then answering each one in your own words, you will be able to internalize the principal points of the book.

A. Why a Global Ethic?

B. The Framework

C. The Fully Functioning Person

D. Way to Wisdom

E. The Good Life

F. A Global Community

A. Why a Global Ethic?

If you could develop a global code of ethics, what would it be?

B. The Framework

Assuming that the promotion of human flourishing is the common ground for the peoples of the world:

1. What is your definition of human flourishing?

2. What factors contribute to human flourishing?

3. What factors thwart human flourishing?

C. The Fully Functioning Person

Assuming that effective leaders in the world community are fully functioning persons, how might you improve your own:

1. Art of Coping

2. Art of Knowing

3. Art of Believing

4. Art of Being

D. Way of Wisdom

Assuming that you are in agreement with the idea of a global ethic, how would you support your position—in the face of opposition? (Make use of all four ways of knowing: personal experience, empirical findings, faith, and reason.)

E. The Good Life

Assume that you have been requested to give the commence-ment address to the graduating class at the International High School. The title of your talk will be "The Good Life: A Global View." What would be the key points of your speech?

F. A Global Community

1. What are the principal attributes of a true citizen of the world?

2. What actions can you take to be an effective citizen of the world?

SUGGESTED READINGS*

- *Birth of a New World: An Open Moment for International Leadership*—Harlan Cleveland.

- *The Future of Mankind*—Karl Jaspers.

- *A Global Ethic: The Declaration of the Parliament of the World's Religions* —edited by Hans Küng and Karl-Josef Kuschel.

- *A Higher Standard of Leadership: Lessons from the Life of Gandhi*—Keshavan Nair.

- *The Moral Sense*—James Q. Wilson.

- *Our Global Neighborhood*—The Commission on Global Governance.

- *Prospects for a Common Morality*—edited by Gene Outka and John Reeder, Jr.

- *Shared Values for a Troubled World*—Rushworth Kidder.

---

*The full citations may be found in the Bibliography.

BIBLIOGRAPHY

Adler, Mortimer. *Truth in Religion: The Plurality of Religions and the Unity of Truth*. New York: Macmillan Publishing Company, 1990.

Alexander, A.L. *Poems That Touch the Heart*. New York: Doubleday, 1956.

Allport, Gordon. *Becoming: Basic Considerations for a Psychology of Personality*. New Haven: Yale University Press, 1955.

Aristotle. *The Nichomachean Ethics*. Buffalo, N.Y.: Prometheus Books, 1987.

Bahá'í International Community. "World Citizenship: A Global Ethic for Sustainable Development." No date given.

Barber, Benjamin, and Patrick Watson. *The Struggle for Democracy*. Boston: Little, Brown and Company, 1988.

Bennis, Warren. *On Becoming a Leader*. Reading, Massachusetts: Addison-Wesley, 1989.

Boutros-Ghali, Boutros. *An Agenda for Peace: Peacemaking and Peace Keeping*. New York: United Nations, 1992.

Bronowski, Jacob. *The Ascent of Man*. Boston: Little, Brown and Company, 1973.

Bronowski, Jacob. *Science and Human Values*. New York: Harper & Row, 1965.

Brown, Noel, and Pierre Quiblier (eds.). *Ethics and Agenda 21*. New York: United Nations, 1994.

Bruner, Jerome. *On Knowing: Essays for the Left Hand*. Cambridge, Mass.: Harvard University Press, 1979.

Buber, Martin. *A Believing Humanism: My Testament, 1902-1965*. New York: Simon and Schuster, 1967.

Buber, Martin. *Between Man and Man*. Boston: Beacon Press, 1955.

Buber, Martin. "Comments on the Idea of Community." In *A Believing Humanism*.

Buber, Martin. "Hebrew Humanism." In *Israel and the World*.

Buber, Martin. *Israel and the World: Essays in a Time of Crisis*. New York: Schocken Books, 1963.

Buber, Martin. *The Legend of the Baal-Shem*. New York: Schocken Books, 1955.

Campbell, Joseph. *The Power of Myth*. New York: Doubleday, 1988.

Cleveland, Harlan. *Birth of a New World: An Open Moment for International Leadership*. San Francisco: Jossey-Bass, 1993.

Commission on Global Governance. *Our Global Neighborhood*. New York: Oxford University Press, 1995.

Council for a Parliament of the World's Religions. "Towards a Global Ethic." Chicago, Illinois, 1993.

Covey, Stephen. *The 7 Habits of Highly Effective People*. New York: Simon and Schuster, 1985.

Dewey, John. *A Common Faith*. New Haven: Yale University Press, 1934.

Dickinson, Emily. "If I Can Stop One Heart From Breaking." In *Poems That Touch the Heart*, compiled by A. L. Alexander.

Douglas, William O. "The Case for Democracy." *The Great Ideas Today—1961*. Edited by Robert Hutchins and Mortimer Adler. Chicago: Encyclopedia Britannica, 1961.

Douglas, William O. *A Living Bill of Rights*. New York: Doubleday & Company, 1961.

Eckhart, Meister. *Meister Eckhart*. Edited by Raymond Blakney. New York: Harper & Row, 1941.

Erasmus, Desiderius. *The Praise of Folly*. Ann Arbor, Michigan: The University of Michigan Press, 1958.

Fadiman, Clifton (ed.). *Living Philosophies: The Reflections of Some Eminent Men and Women of Our Time*. New York: Doubleday, 1990.

Fairley, Barker. *A Study of Goethe*. London: Oxford, 1947.

Feuerbach, Ludwig. *Principles of the Philosophy of the Future*. New York: The Bobbs-Merrill Company, 1966.

Frankl, Viktor. *The Will to Meaning*. Bergenfield, New Jersey: New American Library, 1969.

Fromm, Erich. *Man for Himself*. New York: Henry Holt and Company, 1947.

Fromm, Erich. *To Have Or To Be?* New York: Harper & Row, 1976.

Gandhi, Mahatma. *All Men Are Brothers: Autobiographical Reflections*. New York: Continuum, 1988.

Gandhi, Mahatma. *The Words of Gandhi*. New York: Newmarket Press, 1982.

Gardner, John. "Creating Community in a Pluralistic World." In *Shared Values for a Troubled World*, by Rushworth Kidder.

Gardner, John. *No Easy Victories*. New York: Harper & Row, 1968.

Geneen, Harold. *Managing*. Garden City, N.Y.: Doubleday & Company, 1984.

Gibran, Kahlil. *The Prophet*. New York: Alfred A. Knopf, 1923.

Gordon, Wendell. *The United Nations at the Crossroads of Reform*. Armank, New York: M. E. Sharpe, 1994.

Hamilton, Edith, and Huntington Cairns (eds.). *The Collected Dialogues of Plato*. New York: Bollingen Foundation, 1961.

Hammarskjöld, Dag. Commencement address at Stanford University, Palo Alto, California, June 19, 1955.

Hammarskjöld, Dag. *Markings*. New York: Alfred A. Knopf, 1966.

Hawkins, Peter. "The Spiritual Dimension of the Learning Organization." *Management Education and Development*, Vol. 22, Part 3, 1991.

Hodnett, Edward. *The Art of Problem Solving*. New York: Harper & Brothers, 1955.

Hoffer, Eric. *The True Believer*. New York: Harper & Row, 1951.

Horton, Thomas. *"What Works for Me"*: 16 CEOs Talk About Their Careers and Commitments. New York: Random House, 1986.

James, William. *The Varieties of Religious Experience*. New York: Random House (Modern Library), 1929.

Jaspers, Karl. *Existentialism and Humanism*. New York: Russell F. Moore Company, 1952.

Jaspers, Karl. *The Future of Mankind*. Chicago: The University of Chicago Press, 1961.

Jaspers, Karl. *Kant*. New York: Harcourt, Brace & World, 1962.

Jaspers, Karl. *Philosophy is for Everyman*. New York: Harcourt Brace Jovanovich, 1967.

Jaspers, Karl. "Premises and Possibilities of a New Humanism." In *Existentialism and Humanism*.

Jaspers, Karl. *Way to Wisdom*. New Haven: Yale University Press, 1954.

Kant, Immanuel. *Critique of Pure Reason*. New York: Random House (Modern Library), 1958.

Kant, Immanuel. *Groundwork of the Metaphysics of Morals*. New York: Harper & Row, 1964.

Kelen, Emery (ed.). *Hammarskjöld: The Political Man*. New York: Funk & Wagnalls, 1968.

Kelly, George. *A Theory of Personality: The Psychology of Personal Constructs*. New York: W. W. Norton & Company, 1963.

Kemeny, John. *A Philosopher Looks at Science*. New York: D. VanNostrand Company, 1959.

Kidder, Rushworth. *Shared Values for a Troubled World*. San Francisco: Jossey-Bass Publishers, 1994.

Kierkegaard, Sören. *Purity of Heart Is To Will One Thing*. New York: Harper & Row, 1964.

Kierkegaard, Sören. *Stages on Life's Way*. New York: Schocken Books, 1940.

Kouzes, James, and Barry Posner. *Credibility*. San Francisco: Jossey-Bass, 1993.

Kouzes, James, and Barry Posner. *The Leadership Challenge*. San Francisco: Jossey-Bass, 1987.

Kuhn, Thomas. *The Structure of Scientific Revolutions*. Chicago: University of Chicago Press, 1970.

Küng, Hans. *Global Responsibility: In Search of a New World Ethic*. New York: Crossroad, 1991.

Küng, Hans. *Theology for the Third Millennium*. New York: Doubleday, 1988.

Küng, Hans, and Karl-Josef Kuschel (eds.). *A Global Ethic: The Declaration of the Parliament of the World's Religions*. New York: Continuum, 1993.

Lin, Yutang. *The Wisdom of Confucius*. New York: Random House (Modern Library), 1938.

Little, David. "The Nature and Basis of Human Rights." In *Prospects for a Common Morality*, edited by Gene Outka and John Reeder, Jr.

Machiavelli, Niccolò. *The Prince*. New York: New American Library, 1952.

Maslow, Abraham. *The Psychology of Science*. Chicago: Henry Regnery Company, 1959.

May, Rollo. *The Cry for Myth*. New York: Dell Publishing, 1991.

Mayor, Federico. "A World of Crystal." In *Shared Values for a Troubled World*, edited by Rushworth Kidder.

McGill, Michael, and John Slocum. "Unlearning the Organization." *Organizational Dynamics*, Winter 1994.

McLuhan, Marshall, and Bruce Powers. *The Global Village: Transformations in World Life and Media in the 21st Century*. New York: Oxford University Press, 1989.

Meadows, Donella. *The Global Citizen*. Washington, D.C.: Island Press, 1991.

Moustakas, Clark. *Loneliness and Love*. Englewood Cliffs, New Jersey: Prentice-Hall, 1972.

Moustakas, Clark (ed.). *The Self: Explorations in Personal Growth*. New York: Harper & Row, 1956.

Moyers, Bill. *A World of Ideas I*. New York: Doubleday, 1989.

Moyers, Bill. *A World of Ideas II*. New York: Doubleday, 1990.

Muller, Robert. *The Birth of a Global Civilization*. Anacortes, Washington: World Happiness and Cooperation, 1991.

Murphy, Gardner. *Human Potentialities*. New York: Basic Books, 1958.

Nair, Keshavan. *A Higher Standard of Leadership: Lessons from the Life of Gandhi.* San Francisco: Berrett-Koehler Publishers, 1994.

Nietzsche, Friedrich. *Beyond Good and Evil.* New York: Random House, 1989.

Nussbaum, Martha. *Love's Knowledge: Essays on Philosophy and Literature.* New York: Oxford University Press, 1990.

O'Hara-Devereaux, Mary, and Robert Johansen. *Globalwork: Bridging Distance, Culture & Time.* San Francisco: Jossey-Bass, 1994.

Outka, Gene, and John Reeder, Jr. (eds.). *Prospects for a Common Morality.* Princeton, New Jersey: Princeton University Press, 1993.

Perry, John, and Michael Bratman (eds.). *Introduction to Philosophy.* New York: Oxford University Press, 1993.

Pirsig, Robert. *Lila: An Inquiry into Morals.* New York: Bantam Books, 1991.

Plato. *Theaetetus.* In *The Collected Dialogues of Plato,* edited by Hamilton and Cairns.

Riesman, David. *The Lonely Crowd.* New Haven: Yale University Press, 1961.

Rogers, Carl. *On Becoming a Person.* Boston: Houghton Mifflin Company, 1961.

Rokeach, Milton. *The Nature of Human Values.* New York: The Free Press, 1973.

Russell, Bertrand. *New Hopes for a Changing World.* New York: Minerva Books, 1951.

Russell, Bertrand. *Wisdom of the West.* Garden City, New York: Doubleday & Company, 1959.

Schilpp, Paul Arthur (ed.). *The Philosophy of Karl Jaspers.* New York: Tudor Publishing Company, 1957.

Schilpp, Paul Arthur, and Maurice Friedman (eds.) *The Philosophy of Martin Buber*. LaSalle, Illinois: The Open Court Publishing Company, 1967.

Schweitzer, Albert. *The Decay and Restoration of Civilization*. London: Black, 1929.

Schweitzer, Albert. *Memoirs of Childhood and Youth*. New York: Macmillan Company, 1955.

Schweitzer, Albert. *Out of My Life and Thought: An Autobiography*. New York: Holt, Rinehart and Winston, 1961.

Schweitzer, Albert. *The Philosophy of Civilization*. Buffalo, New York: Prometheus Books, 1987.

Senge, Peter. *The Fifth Discipline: The Art & Practice of the Learning Organization*. New York: Doubleday/Currency, 1990.

Shute, Stephen, and Susan Hurley (eds.). *On Human Rights: The Oxford Amnesty Lectures*. New York: Basic Books, 1993.

Smith, Huston. *The World's Religions*. New York: Harper Collins, 1991.

Tarnas, Richard. *The Passion of the Western Mind: Understanding the Ideas That Have Shaped Our World View*. New York: Harmony Books, 1991.

Tillich, Paul. *The Courage To Be*. New Haven: Yale University Press, 1952.

Tillich, Paul. *Dynamics of Faith*. New York: Harper & Row, 1958.

Tivnan, Edward. *The Moral Imagination: Confronting the Ethical Issues of Our Day*. New York: Simon & Schuster, 1995.

Versényi, Laszlo. *Socratic Humanism*. Yale University Press, 1963.

Walker, Barbara (ed.). *Uniting the Peoples and Nations: Readings in World Federalism*. Washington, D.C.: World Federalist Association and Amsterdam: World Federalist Movement, 1993.

Weber, Max. *The Methodology of the Social Sciences*. New York: The Free Press, 1949.

Wheelis, Allen. *The Quest for Identity*. New York: W. W. Norton & Company, 1958.

Williams, Bernard. *Ethics and the Limits of Philosophy*. Cambridge, Massachusetts: Harvard University Press, 1985.

Willkie, Wendell. *One World*. Urbana, Illinois: University of Illinois Press, 1943.

Wilson, Francis. "Human Nature and Aesthetic Growth." In *The Self*, edited by Clark Moustakas.

Wilson, James Q. *The Moral Sense*. New York: The Free Press, 1993.

NAME INDEX

Adler, Mortimer, 44, 167, 169
Alexander, A.L., 123, 167-168
Allport, Gordon, 167
Aristotle, 28, 70, 96, 99, 167

Barber, Benjamin, 167
Bellah, Robert, 150-151
Bennis, Warren, 35, 167
Blakney, Raymond, 169
Boutros-Ghali, Boutros, 167
Bratman, Michael, 30, 173
Bronowski, Jacob, 133, 167-168
Bruner, Jerome, 168
Buber, Martin, 16, 31, 115-116,
123, 131, 168, 174
Buddha, 72, 128

Cairns, Huntington, 170, 173
Campbell, Joseph, 25, 129, 168
Church, F. Forrester, 14
Churchill, Winston, 142
Cleveland, Harlan, 165, 168
Confucius, 55, 72, 128, 172

Covey, Stephen, 168
Dewey, John, 168
Dickinson, Emily, 123
Douglas, William O., 145

Eckhart, Meister, 4, 169
Erasmus, Desiderius, 145, 169

Fackenheim, Emil, 116
Fadiman, Clifton, 75, 169
Fairley, Barker, 169
Feuerbach, Ludwig, 169
Frankl, Viktor, 169
Franklin, Benjamin, 71
Friedman, Milton, 116, 174
Fromm, Erich, 72, 96, 144, 169

Gandhi, Mahatma, vii, 25, 27,
82, 96, 114, 128, 141-142, 155,
165, 169, 173
Gardner, John, 47
Geneen, Harold, 51-52, 169
Gibran, Kahlil, 69, 81, 169

177

Goethe, Johann Wolfgang, 169
Gordon, Wendell, 167, 170

Hamilton, Edith, 170, 173
Hammarskjöld, Dag, 137, 170
Hawkins, Peter, 170
Hesburgh, Father Theodore, 112
Hodnett, Edward, 49, 170
Hoffer, Eric, 71, 134, 170
Horton, Thomas, 112, 170
Hurley, Susan, 174

Isaiah, 150

James, William, 23. 147-149
Jaspers, Karl, iii, xv, 1, 8, 13, 16, 20, 28, 90, 99-100, 165, 170, 173
Jesus, 72, 128
Johansen, Robert, 173

Kant, Immanuel, xiii, 13, 26, 28, 82-83, 87, 90,99, 101, 147, 170-171
Kelen, Emery, 171
Kelly, George, 85
Kemeny, John, 93, 171
Kidder, Rushworth, 104, 165, 169, 171-172
Kierkegaard, Sören, 70, 94, 171
Kirkpatrick, Jeane, 75
Kouzes, James, 108, 123, 171
Kuhn, Thomas, 171
Küng, Hans, 165
Kuschel, Karl-Josef, 165, 171

Lewin, Kurt, ix
Lin, Yutang, 172

Lincoln, Abraham, 54
Little, David, 172

Machiavelli, Niccolò, 108, 116, 172
Maslow, Abraham, 87-88, 117, 146, 172
May, Rollo, 172
Mayor, Federico, 172
McGill, Michael, 63, 172
McLuhan, Marshall, 6, 172
Meadows, Donella, 172
Moses, 128
Moustakas, Clark, 78, 172, 175
Moyers, Bill, 14, 151, 172
Muhammad, 26, 72, 128
Muller, Robert, 172
Murphy, Gardner, 172

Nair, Keshavan, vii, 155, 165, 173
Nietzsche, Friedrich, 14, 33, 173
Nussbaum, Martha, 173

O'Hara-Devereaux, Mary, 173
Oracle at Delphi, 61, 74
Outka, Gene, 165, 172-173

Perry, John, 30
Plato, 28, 58, 72, 96, 98-99, 170, 173
Posner, Barry, 108, 123, 171
Powers, Bruce, 172

Reeder, John Jr., 165, 172-173
Riesman, David, 74, 173
Rogers, Carl, 119-120, 122, 173
Rokeach, Milton, 65-68, 71, 173

Russell, Bertrand, 21, 65, 170, 173

Schilpp, Paul Arthur, 116, 173-174
Schweitzer, Albert, viii, 114
Seneca, viii, 114
Senge, Peter, 76, 118, 136, 174
Shute, Stephen, 174
Slocum, John, 63, 172
Smith, Huston, 24
Socrates, 20, 28, 36-41, 66, 72, 96, 98-100, 103-104, 106, 128, 154

Tarnas, Richard, x, 11, 174
Thomas, Ralph, 92
Tillich, Paul, 73-74, 95, 174
Tivnan, Edward, 174

Versényi, Laszlo, 174

Walker, Barbara, 174
Watson, Patrick, 167
Weber, Max, 92, 175
Wheelis, Allen, 95, 175
Williams, Bernard, 103-104, 175
Willkie, Wendell, 175
Wilson, Francis, 175
Wilson, James Q., 105, 165

SUBJECT INDEX

Art of Being, 72–79
Art of Believing, 65–72
Art of Coping, 47–55
Art of Knowing, 55–65
Art of Living, 44–47

Bahá'í International
Community, 135

citizens of the world, xiv,
134–138
code of ethics, 105
Commission on Global
Governance, 168
common ethic, 150–154
common ground, 2–4
communication, 115–118
community, 131–132
compassion, 119–123
contribution, 113–115
cooperation, 123–127
core learning disciplines, 136
Council for a Parliament of the
World's Religions, 6

daily life, 17–20
Declaration of Human Rights,
138
democracy, 141–145
dialogue, 115–118
dual citizenship, 135, 137–138,
154

evil, xiv, 128
experience, 87–90

faith, 94–98
fully functioning person, 35–80

global citizen, 134–138
global community, 129–154
Golden Rule, 111
good, xiv, 128
good life, 103–128

helping relationships, 119–123
hope, 130–131
human flourishing, xii, 31
humanitas, xiii, 31

Humanitas, xiii, xiv, 31–43
integrity, 108–112
I-Thou, 116

leader, xiii, 34, 40, 102, 128,
    149, 154
leadership, vii, xiv, 126
leap of faith, 94
lifelong learning, 56

mental models, 85–87, 136
moral equivalent of war, 147
myth, 25

nihilism, 14, 16, 33

objective truth, 97
observation, 91–94

paradigm, 33–34, 96
peace, 145–150
personal mastery, 136
philosophy, 28–31
problem solving, 48–49

reason, 98–101
religion, 24–27
responsibilities, 140–141
rights, 138–140

science, 21–24
shared vision, 136
subjective truth, 97
systems thinking, 76, 136

team learning, 136
team member, 124
Temple of Goodness, 106–108
Temple of Hope, 132–134
Temple of Human Potential,
    41–44
Temple of Humanity, 13–17
Temple of Wisdom, 83–85
True Believer, 71
truth, 82–83, 85, 102

ultimate concern, 95
United Nations, 138, 148
universal values, 104–105

value system, 66
values, 65–71

Weltanschauung, 17, 32
wisdom, 83–84, 102
world government, 7
world view, xii, 3, 11–34